Doing Business Anywhere

The Essential Guide to Going Global

Tom Travis

BICENTENNIAL
1807
WILEY
2007
BICENTENNIAL

John Wiley & Sons, Inc.

Published by John Wiley & Sons, Inc., Hoboken, New Jersey.
Published simultaneously in Canada.

Wiley Bicentennial Logo: Richard J. Pacifico

For general information on our other products and services or for technical support,
please contact our Customer Care Department within the United States at
(800) 762-2974, outside the United States at (317) 572-3993 or fax (317) 572-4002.

Wiley also publishes its books in a variety of electronic formats. Some content that
appears in print may not be available in electronic books. For more information about
Wiley products, visit our web site at www.wiley.com.

Library of Congress Cataloging-in-Publication Data:

Travis, Tom, 1947–
  Doing business anywhere: the essential guide to going global / Tom Travis.
     p.   cm.
  Includes bibliographical references.
  ISBN-13: 978-0-471-97317-1 (cloth)
1. International business enterprises—Management. I. Title.
  HD62.4.T735   2007
  658'.049—dc22

                                                        2006101141

Printed in the United States of America.

10 9 8 7 6 5 4 3 2 1

To my parents, Louis and Corrine Travis,
and my sister Cathy

CONTENTS

FOREWORD

I have had the pleasure of knowing and working closely with Tom Travis for over 20 years. Tom and his firm were key business partners with me while I was associated with both Sara Lee Corporation (now Hanesbrands Inc.) and Russell Corporation. They provided advice and guidance that was unmatched in the industry. Among Tom's greatest assets are the personal relationships he has formed around the globe. When we entered new international markets, I would seek advice from Tom. With his intimate knowledge and relationships, he has always steered me to business partners who not only were technically competent, but even more important, shared the same strong values and business ethics.

When I first read Tom's book, I was intrigued. Nowhere else had I encountered a book that boiled down the essence of what every businessperson needs to know about global trade into one easily accessible resource. In *Doing Business Anywhere*, Tom has isolated six Tenets of Global Trade that are universal to every global trader.

Doing Business Anywhere doesn't pull any punches. As Tom points out in Chapter 2, if you are going to compete in a cutthroat global marketplace, you are going to have to understand trade agreements, how they work, and how to get the most out of what they have to offer. Chapter 3, entitled "Protect Your Brand at All Costs" was the chapter I found most illuminating. The pull to segregate the myriad aspects of brand management into different divisions with different agendas might at first seem like a logical way to proceed. After reading this chapter, it became abundantly clear how intellectual property rights, the decisions a company makes with respect to labor and environmental issues in the context of sourcing decisions and forming strategic partnerships, and the way you communicate your company's vision all are part and parcel of the same thing: keeping your company's most valuable asset—its brand—safe and strong.

Chapter 4, which covers ethics in international business, takes the concept of protecting your brand one step further. As Tom explains, ethical behavior in business really is not only the right thing to do, it is the smart way to conduct international business. I am proud to say that my company had a strong ethical business culture, and I encourage anyone delving into the global trade arena to read this chapter with care. Corporate governance is fast becoming one of the most important aspects of a company's overall value. The advice Tom gives is worth its weight in gold.

As for the subject covered in Chapter 5, "Stay Secure in an Insecure World," Tom and his firm really are experts in this area. Since the September 11 attacks on U.S. soil, governments worldwide have banded together with the private sector to keep international borders safe for commerce and travel. And the other aspects of security often overlooked—cargo security and the personal security of globe-trotting executives, staff, and their families—are addressed in a way that should make every reader reexamine his or her internal policies.

Chapter 6, "Expect the Unexpected," is so true. If you think it won't happen to you . . . well, it will. Tom lays out some excellent examples of how forces beyond your control can slow your operations down or even bring them to a halt. His tips for handling potential crises are invaluable. You might want to keep a copy of these tips in your procedures manual.

In remarking how "All Global Business Is Personal" in Chapter 7, Tom once again hits the nail on the head. Forming close personal ties with colleagues and clients is always a good way to go regardless of where you transact business, but its importance is magnified when you are doing business across continents and cultures.

Finally, Tom ties it all up with the concept that transparency really is the glue that holds all these Tenets of Global Trade together. In the twenty-first century global business environment, transparency is much more than a buzzword, it is essential to operating in a world where compliance with complex trade rules, oversight of transcontinental supply chains, and strict adherence to security protocols are absolute requirements for global business success.

The world of global trade is constantly evolving. No one treatise is going to tell you everything you need to know about how to conduct your particular business abroad. What Tom has done in *Doing Business Anywhere* is to offer the most important emerging trends in international business. The Tenets of Global Trade are the starting point, the foundation for transacting business abroad. Without a firm understanding of these guiding principles, everything else is pointless.

JACK WARD
Chairman and CEO, Russell Corporation (Retired)

PREFACE

Whether we like it or not, we all now play a part in the new global marketplace. That cup of coffee you sip in the morning is brewed from beans grown in Colombia, Brazil, or Jamaica. Your suit says "Made in Italy," even though the wool came from sheep sheared in New Zealand and the zippers hail from factories in Japan. Your American brand sedan sports a muffler made in Canada, a steering wheel from Spain, and ignition wiring produced in the Philippines. You work on a personal computer assembled in Mexico with parts coming from the United States, Thailand, and China.

From the food you eat, to the clothes you wear, to the conveyances you ride in, and the technology tools you use to navigate the information highway, you are already actively involved in global trade.

The impact of global trade is, of course, not limited to U.S. consumers. In Brazil, housewives purchase laundry detergent made by corporate giant Procter & Gamble from a Wal-Mart Supercenter in Sao Paolo. Kids in Costa Rica text message each other using American cell phones and families in Antigua place their Christmas gifts under trimmed trees grown in Florida. Hungry Hong Kong shoppers might step into a McDonald's for a burger and super-sized fries; and don't be surprised if during a business trip to Taiwan you pass a KFC jam-packed with patrons enjoying finger-lickin' good chicken. There are Starbucks in Singapore, Disney theme parks in Hong Kong and France, and cinema houses in Kenya showing the latest Hollywood action films.

As the politicians and pundits ponder the wisdom and efficacy of globalization on cable news talk shows and on the floors of Congress, forward-thinking businesspeople have moved beyond talking and are taking action. They are exploring the opportunities global trade offers at home and abroad.

Each time a civilization shifts—be it from an agrarian society to an industrialized one or from a manufacturing economy to one of globalization fueled by the new age of information—there are those who understandably bemoan the growing pains that come with these shifts and those who look for opportunities in the new economic landscape. If you are reading this book, chances are you fall into the latter category.

Global business can mean many things to many people. In my assessment, the essence of global business is the movement of goods, ideas, and capital across borders. It means gaining cooperation among individuals and businesses so that they are aligned to execute within a global context.

In my more than 30 years as an active participant in the global marketplace, I've thought about the principles that have become universal to the achievement of global business success. I have isolated six Tenets of Global Trade that increasingly will guide successful entrepreneurs as they explore the opportunities of the twenty-first century global marketplace. These Tenets are set out in the pages of this book.

This book is not designed as a primer for importing, exporting, or setting up a consultancy practice or a manufacturing operation abroad. It won't provide tips for procuring international finance or advice on how to streamline your global supply chain or develop state-of-the-art distribution channels. The myriad complexities and issues connected with these trading topics are country, industry, and economy specific and treatises covering these discrete topics abound.

What this book does offer you is a bird's-eye view of the landscape of global trade. The emerging trends set forth in its pages—The Tenets of Global Trade—provide guideposts for your journey as you expand your business globally. It is my hope that these tools to doing business anywhere help you achieve prosperity on a global scale.

Tom Travis

Miami, Florida
January 2007

ACKNOWLEDGMENTS

A book such as this is always a collaborative effort. I am grateful to the partners, principals, associates, and trade advisors of both Sandler, Travis & Rosenberg, PA and Sandler & Travis Trade Advisory Services for helping to illuminate and solidify the concepts that eventually became the subject of this manuscript.

First and foremost I want to recognize and thank my law partner, Nancy Wollin, for her immense and critical contributions to this manuscript. Simply put, this book would not have been possible without her. At every single stage from my initial thoughts and concepts for the book and its themes to the final drafting, redrafting, and editing, Nancy was not only a knowledgeable sounding board, helpful critic, and spectacular writer, researcher, and editor, but also an inspiration, catalyst, coconspirator, and friend. Our brainstorming sessions at which we defined, debated, and further refined the message and themes represented the creative process at its best. This teamwork was not only something that was unique and special, but it was an experience that I will always treasure and one that I can only hope to equal sometime in the future. Thank you Nancy!!

I have been extremely fortunate throughout my career to have Lee Sandler as my partner. Lee is a brilliant attorney, an effective strategist and tactician, and a kind and compassionate man. He embodies everything I admire in a lawyer and value in a friend. Whatever the issue, Lee has the unique ability to isolate and distinguish between major and minor problems and, more important, to place seemingly insurmountable legal disputes and questions into their proper context. He fights hard for our clients, but he always fights fair. Because of this, he has earned the respect and admiration of clients and adversaries alike. Even after 30 years, he continues to amaze me with his steadfast integrity and unwavering kindness. I am a better lawyer, a better businessman, and a better person for knowing Lee.

I also want to take this opportunity to recognize Len Rosenberg. Throughout his 25-year association with the firm, Len has taken on the critical role of anchor to our many business enterprises and initiatives. Not only is Len an excellent attorney, but he has remained devoted to one of the cardinal principles of business: the importance of the bottom line.

Sandler, Travis & Rosenberg and Sandler & Travis Trade Advisory Services' Chief Operating Officer Kimberlee Mark defines the term "stick-to-itiveness." When I first considered writing this book, Kimberlee was one of the first people I consulted. She has a keen intelligence and an uncanny ability to see the big picture while taking care to ensure that the smallest of details are addressed. The truth is that if this project had not passed Kimberlee's litmus test, I'm not sure that I would have taken it on. I cannot thank her enough for her contributions not only to the successful completion of this book, but also to the continued success of the firms.

Shawn McCausland also contributed greatly to this book by providing research and editorial assistance. Shawn has a keen eye for detail and never ceases to amaze me with his encyclopedic knowledge of trade matters. He is dedicated, thorough, and a professional of the highest order.

Also, Haydee Perdomo and Ivon Ros worked diligently under tight deadlines to put the manuscript in good order.

The many talented and creative global entrepreneurs that I have been fortunate to represent as clients, and in many instances have been even more fortunate to count as lifelong friends, were an inspiration for this book. While they are too numerous to list, I do want to offer special thanks to Jerry Cook not only for his insights and perspective, but for being a constant reminder that one can enjoy global business success while still retaining one's humanity. Jerry represents everything I admire in a successful businessman. He is thoughtful, intelligent, and above all, a man of principle whose deeds set an example we should all emulate. If anyone provides a moral compass for how to succeed in twenty-first century global business, it is Jerry.

Finally, I want to thank my agent Celia Rocks and her partner Dottie DeHart of Rocks-DeHart Public Relations, as well as the editorial team at John Wiley & Sons for their encouragement and support.

ABOUT THE AUTHOR

Tom Travis is managing partner of Sandler, Travis & Rosenberg, PA, a leading international trade and customs law firm. He also serves as the chairman of Sandler & Travis Trade Advisory Services, which provides management services on customs compliance and security matters for global companies. Mr. Travis has extensive experience in a wide variety of international trade and customs matters, including the representation of countries and private interests in matters before the World Trade Organization (WTO), the World Customs Organization (WCO), the U.S. Congress, and federal agencies, and before the revenue and customs services of many nations. He has played a leading role in the firm's trade policy and government relations group, which has provided services to governments and major trade associations in many countries, including the Republic of Korea, Cambodia, Pakistan, Singapore, Sri Lanka, Malaysia, U.A.E., Haiti, Fiji, the Dominican Republic, Turkey, El Salvador, China, Colombia, Laos, Guatemala, the Philippines, and Indonesia.

Mr. Travis is widely recognized as a leading authority in the complex and highly technical world of international trade. He possesses extensive knowledge on subjects such as the classification, valuation, and origin of imported merchandise, preference systems, and free trade agreements between the United States and its trading partners. Mr. Travis is a distinguished speaker on topics ranging from international business ethics and social responsibility in sourcing to technical aspects of free trade agreements and import/export law.

Both Sandler, Travis & Rosenberg, PA, and Sandler & Travis Trade Advisory Services are prominent industry leaders due to the extraordinary depth of talent and experience possessed by their staff. Mr. Travis has been instrumental in attracting professional resources to the firms, including two former U.S. Ambassadors and Chief Textile Negotiators, a former Commissioner and five former Deputy Commissioners of U.S. Customs (the second highest Customs position in the United States), and other senior professionals from the Office of the United States Trade Representative; U.S. Customs and Border Protection; and the State, Labor, and Commerce Departments. The foundation of the firms' success is built on providing governments, multinationals, manufacturers, importers, exporters, and retailers the information and support they require to meet the constantly changing demands of global trade. The firms host more than 100 seminars per year and publish online newsletters, bulletins, and technical reports to assist clients in the development of their strategic planning and compliance efforts. The firms have 10 offices throughout the United States and in Canada, South America and Asia staffed by over 300 customs and trade professionals.

Mr. Travis is an honors graduate of Princeton University (AB, 1969) and Columbia University Law School (JD,

1972), and he is also a member of the Washington, DC;
Florida; New York; and New Jersey Bar Associations.

Telephone: (305) 267-9200
Fax: (305) 267-5155
E-mail: ttravis@strtrade.com
www.strtrade.com

THE TENETS OF GLOBAL TRADE: EMERGING TRENDS IN INTERNATIONAL BUSINESS

We have all heard that the world is flat. And while that may be true, the world is also very, very large, with many divergent peoples, cultures, languages, borders, and customs. Since business is increasingly global, entrepreneurs must organize, plan, operate, and execute in new ways. The complexity of this multilayered, multidimensional environment is magnified by the fact that all international transactions are populated by many independent, but indispensable, parties that must communicate and coordinate to successfully import, export, or enter new markets. Add to this mix, the conflicting and confusing laws and regulations of many nations, and it becomes clear that doing business internationally is certainly complicated and subject to greater risk.

Given that, are there any themes or principles that cut across different business models, industries, and products to guide international businesspersons through this uneven and difficult terrain?

Based on my experience as an advisor to global entrepreneurs, multinational companies, and the governments of developing nations, I believe that the answer is yes. There are several tenets and emerging themes that cannot only provide guideposts and danger signals, but that also are absolutely essential to successfully navigating the international business environment in which we and our children will operate. Ignoring any of these tenets can prove detrimental to your international enterprise, but embracing them will certainly broaden your understanding of exactly what it takes to be successful in our new world economy. I have termed these principles the Tenets of Global Trade because they apply to all international business pursuits, regardless of country, commodity, or culture. These Tenets are:

- ♦ Take advantage of trade agreements: think outside the border.
- ♦ Protect your brand at all costs.
- ♦ Maintain high ethical standards.
- ♦ Stay secure in an insecure world.
- ♦ Expect the unexpected.
- ♦ All global business is personal.

Let's examine these Tenets.

TAKE ADVANTAGE OF TRADE AGREEMENTS: THINK OUTSIDE THE BORDER

As commerce continues to globalize and competition among nations increases, many governments seek special advantages with selected countries through bilateral and multilateral trade agreements and preference programs. These mechanisms provide competitive advantages by eliminating barriers and customs duties for products and services produced in countries that have implemented such trade pacts. Therefore, by their very nature, these agreements often provide opportunities for those knowledgeable and creative enough to bend them to their advantage. Companies participating in such negotiations and those that scrutinize the details usually end up winning. Those that don't frequently lose their competitive edge.

PROTECT YOUR BRAND AT ALL COSTS

You must protect your own brand at all costs. Often the most valuable asset a company has is the intelligence and creativity that defines its uniqueness. Protecting these sorts of assets across borders is hard enough, but protecting your company's reputation in the court of world opinion may be an even more critical mission. If you don't take care of your brand and its reputation, not much else matters.

MAINTAIN HIGH ETHICAL STANDARDS

Good ethics always make good business sense, but this is even more so in a global context, where it can be extremely difficult to remedy missteps that occur across continents. Increasingly, multinational companies from the developed world are exporting core values to their own operations and business partners in countries around the globe. This "exported product" may be required by law or convention. But regardless of its origin, the importance of adhering to business ethics lies in the fact that they increase accountability and simplify the communication of standards.

The establishment of core values not only defines a company and its employees, but it can also encourage and influence its global business partners and the countries in which they operate. This type of message can overlap and transcend different peoples, cultures, and business perspectives. Successful companies embrace this new reality. Now the financial markets recognize and reward it.

STAY SECURE IN AN INSECURE WORLD

An obvious consequence for businesses as a result of the tragedy of September 11, 2001, is the mandate from government to illuminate, identify, and secure each step and partner in a company's international supply chain. This is to ensure that weapons of mass destruction or other dangerous cargo is detected before it reaches our shores. While there are costs associated with this new obligation, there is emerging evidence of the benefits, not only to security, but also to the bottom line. Increasingly, companies are finding that measures adopted to improve security also help improve efficiencies in areas such as inventory management and loss prevention. This realignment also enhances business operations and communication among the diverse group of entities through which imported goods are brought to domestic markets. In short, new security requirements provide transparency, which is good for the government and good for business.

EXPECT THE UNEXPECTED

Companies everywhere must deal with uncertainties and events that are not set forth in traditional business plans. The global context of commerce today magnifies geometrically the number and classes of occurrences and events that can disrupt the finest business models. Whether the event creates opportunity or peril, how you prepare and plan to react to the unexpected must become an essential part of your global strategy.

ALL GLOBAL BUSINESS IS PERSONAL

How do you ensure execution and commonality of purpose in a multinational context in which you don't own or control all the elements of your supply chain? Legal action in the international context is uncertain and slow at best. Therefore, in a world where you cannot resort to quick legal actions to resolve disputes, the answer is to forge strategic personal relationships with all the different players that are part of your global alliance. Such personal relationships, especially among the top leaders of your alliance partners, foster communication, reliability, and the informal consultation that can attenuate problems long before they become disputes. More importantly, these relationships frequently result in innovations and reconfigurations that can lead to greater success.

HOW THE TENETS CAME ABOUT

I came to formulate the Tenets of Global Trade during the 30 years I have been engaged as an international trade attorney and global business advisor. The story of my firm's longstanding involvement with a group of forward-thinking entrepreneurs and their push for a developing nation's emergence into the global trade arena illustrates how the application of these universal themes converged to create great business success.

Emergence on the Global Stage

On a typical muggy day in Hong Kong in 1994, we received a phone call from Chinese entrepreneur Christopher Cheng inviting me and my colleague Bill Houston to join him for breakfast at the Ritz Carlton Hotel in the island's bustling Central district. The Ritz Carlton is one of Cheng's numerous worldwide real estate holdings, and as I was being seated at his usual table overlooking Victoria Harbour, the beautiful surroundings served as a nice reminder that all this grueling international business travel sometimes does have its perks.

Cheng is an Asian business powerhouse. As executive chairman of USI Holdings Limited and managing director of Wing Tai Corporation Ltd., Cheng's business interests involve worldwide apparel manufacture and distribution, real estate development and management, hospitality management services, and securities investment. It was the apparel part of his global enterprise that he wanted to discuss over breakfast, in particular, a venture he was pursuing for Wing Tai. Wing Tai was already known as a renowned apparel company throughout Asia. The company manufactures clothing for some of the world's most recognizable brands and Cheng had a well-established reputation for creating opportunities where others might see only obstacles.

As the waitress poured our first cups of tea, Cheng got right to the point. He wanted to talk about Cambodia.

In the mid-1990s, Cambodia was not even a blip on most international traders' radar screens. The impoverished country had survived the devastating Pol Pot regime, where millions of its people had fallen victim to brutal executions, starvation, and disease, only to become mired in a decade-long civil war following the Vietnamese invasion in 1978. Even though some semblance of peace had entered the Cambodian landscape by the mid-1990s due to the intervention of U.N. peacekeeping forces and the promulgation of a new constitution, the country was still struggling with finding its pathway to stability. I waited with anticipation to find out why a man like Cheng would have set his sights on this orphan of Southeast Asia.

Cheng explained that his enterprise had opened a small trousers manufacturing plant outside of Phnom Penh. The Cambodian workers were eager and industrious and had a talent for producing quality goods at a competitive price. Cambodia seemed like a great place to develop apparel manufacturing because it was not yet operating under the quota system that restricted apparel exports to the United States. Whenever you limit the amount of exports by any quota, you limit supply, thereby making quota itself a commodity. This artificially increases the price of apparel. The absence of these restrictive quotas would provide the Cambodian market with a competitive advantage over its neighbors because manufacturers and

U.S. importers would not be forced to bear these additional artificial costs.

Despite these cost advantages, the Cambodian factory could not sell its products to the lucrative U.S. marketplace. Lingering and outdated U.S. trade policies regarding Southeast Asia in general and Cambodia in particular were interfering with Cheng's plans to establish a stronghold of apparel manufacturing in Phnom Penh.

A U.S. embargo against Cambodia had been lifted in 1992, but barriers to trade between Cambodia and the United States still existed. While imports into the United States from Cambodia were not outright prohibited, the country did not enjoy most-favored-nation (MFN) status. (MFN is now referred to as normal trade relations or NTR.) That meant that duty rates for apparel imports from Cambodia could hover near 90 percent, while imports of identical garments manufactured in almost every other Asian country carried duty rates in the range of 15 to 22 percent. Duty rates for apparel are calculated on the value of a garment, so a 90 percent duty imposed on a $10 article of clothing resulted in a duty liability of $9. There was no way that a Cambodian manufacturer could compete in the U.S. market when the cost to import goods was almost equal to the cost of their manufacture.

Emerging Trends in Trade

This brilliant Chinese entrepreneur, Bill, and I spent the better part of the next two hours designing a plan for Cambodia that would end up not only changing the course of U.S. trade relations in that part of the world, but would set off a series of chain reactions affecting international labor standards and other ethical principles of trade. As we formulated solutions to this trade dilemma and as our plan progressed over the years through the complex maze that defines global trade relations, I began to see several important trade trends emerging. I termed these trends the Tenets of Global Trade because they are universal principles for success in the international business arena that cut across industries and geography to drive the global entrepreneur to success. The story of Cambodia's entry into the global trade community embodies each of these guiding principles for success in international business.

Opening Up Opportunities

Once we decided to move full steam ahead toward making Cambodia an apparel manufacturing hub, our first order of business was to find a way to lower duty rates on Cambodian goods so in-country manufacturers could offer products to the U.S. market at competitive prices. We started the wheels rolling in Congress through intense lobbying efforts. Republican Senator John McCain, a decorated Vietnam War veteran, sponsored legislation normalizing trade relations with Cambodia. His support, along with that of others, stemmed from a belief that the war-torn nation needed industry and economic growth to sustain a lasting peace. And the quickest way to achieve that goal was to open the country to the U.S. market. In October of 1996, Cambodia was granted MFN status.

The success of this tariff realignment exceeded expectations. Before long, major U.S. companies were placing production in Cambodia. A leader in this Cambodian apparel expansion was The Gap, which was seeking new factories in which to place orders for its recently introduced Old Navy stores. Old Navy is known for selling quality clothing at lower prices, and the only way to meet customer expectations was to find a venue in which to produce these goods for less money. Cambodia, which now promised low-cost labor and quality workmanship, and had no real trade restrictions with the United States, seemed ideal. Unlike The Gap's other manufacturing sources in Asia, Cambodia was not yet regulated by quota. This advantage soon caught the eye of other manufacturers and retailers and Cambodia's exports to the United States increased from $2.4 million in 1996 to $361.7 million in 1998, and nearly all of these exports were apparel. For the 12-month period ending in October 2006, the total was approaching $2.1 billion. Trade legislation had once again opened up a new market.

Both Cheng and The Gap had embraced an important Tenet of Global Trade. They had dared to think outside the border and take advantage of trade agreements. By looking to Cambodia in the first place, Cheng made the decision to aggressively pursue business opportunities in a location where trade barriers existed. And when he encountered a tariff barrier to open and free trade, he crossed it by changing the status quo. The Gap seized a new trading opportunity in a location that had provided it a competitive edge. By keeping abreast of the evolution of trade negotiations and new laws affecting tariffs, the company was able to seize the moment and enhance the value of its assets while blazing a new trail for American buyers and Cambodian factories.

Even seemingly perfect situations are never static when it comes to global trade. This Cambodian edge— the lack of quotas—did not escape the powerful domestic U.S. textiles lobby. As U.S. industry saw Cambodia's exports rise in this important sector, they lobbied the U.S.

government to cap these exports by imposing restrictive quotas and limiting Cambodia's rapid growth. Before long, the U.S. government decided to heed the industry's demands and impose quotas on textile and apparel exports from Cambodia. This time it was the government of Cambodia, along with the factory owners, that called on our firm to help negotiate trade terms with the United States.

How we came to represent the government of Cambodia in these negotiations was also the result of embracing an important Tenet of Global Trade: All global business is personal. This opportunity came up by virtue of the long-standing relationships our firm had forged in Asia. As this tenet reflects, it is the personal touch that makes all the difference in establishing meaningful international business relationships. While developing trust and mutual reliance with strategic partners, customers, and clients is critical in all business models, it is particularly crucial in international business where geography, culture, language, different laws, and the uncertain enforcement of rights and responsibilities are present.

Forging Lasting Relationships

When I first starting traveling to Asia in the early 1980s, I was fortunate to make the acquaintance of Henry Tang, then the chairman of Peninsula Knitters, a prominent Hong Kong sweater manufacturer. Today, Tang holds the position of Financial Secretary for the Government of Hong Kong, one of the most senior positions in the Special Administrative Region's government. Tang and his company had become a client and over the years we had developed not only a close business relationship, but a friendship as well. As we got to know each other, we would often discuss the growing emergence, importance, and complexity of the China-U.S. relationship. Early on, he gave me some sobering but important advice. He said that gaining the confidence of the Chinese business community would take at least 10 years. In order to build a foundation in Asia for real success, I would need to demonstrate that I was a reliable and valued partner over the long haul.

Tang was absolutely right. Gaining the confidence of this group that controlled so much of the world's soft goods manufacturing did not come easy. But through my frequent trips to Asia to service clients and build the firm's book of business in the region, this dynamic group of entrepreneurs and I got to know each other well. Over time, a mutual trust and admiration was built that benefits the firm and, I believe, our clients to this day.

Slightly more than 10 years after receiving Tang's sage advice, I was summoned to the Grand Stanford Hotel in Kowloon to attend a meeting convened by then Cambodian Minister of Commerce Cham Prasidh. The purpose of the meeting, populated in large part by powerful Chinese businessmen with interests in Cambodia, was to engage a law firm to represent Cambodia's interests in the upcoming quota negotiations with the United States. The decision on who to hire and how to proceed with the negotiations was critical not only to these businessmen, but to the Cambodian people who, for the first time, were finding employment and a degree of prosperity as participants in global trade.

Minister Prasidh went around the room and asked each of these powerful Chinese business representatives whether they would support engaging Sandler, Travis & Rosenberg for this important task. Without reservation each responded affirmatively and we were hired. This was the moment that I knew the friendships developed with these individuals and the professional work my firm had provided to them really had blossomed into the kind of personal relationships that are essential for international entrepreneurs in the global age. These gentlemen had come to know me on a personal level as well as a professional one. The years of traveling to Asia to nurture these relationships had culminated in my firm being chosen for this important engagement. The decision was quick and unanimous, but it was years in the making.

Doing the Right Thing

The negotiations regarding how much quota Cambodia would be afforded were critical to the nascent industry's continued viability. Too little quota and factories would have to shut down, resulting in huge losses to the companies that had invested in Cambodia's apparel industry infrastructure and quashing the dreams of thousands of workers who now relied on factory jobs for their livelihood. As the negotiations heated up, the U.S. government posited an unorthodox and, for the times, unheard of and unexpected quid pro quo. It proposed to create a direct link between the amount of quota allocated to Cambodia and labor protections for Cambodian workers. It also insisted that Cambodia work closely with the U.N.-sponsored International Labor Organization (ILO) to ensure that Cambodia enforced internationally recognized labor standards. This was the first time in history that a country's trade benefits were to be linked to progress on labor rights. Our first reaction was to recommend strongly to Minister Prasidh that he reject the proposal out of hand. No other country had ever been given this type of ultimatum and by accepting it, Cambodia would find itself at a distinct disadvantage. Minister Prasidh listened carefully to the U.S. government's proposal and to our advice. He and I retired to a private room to discuss the matter further and it was then that I came to understand three of the Tenets of Global Trade: Expect the unexpected, maintain high ethical standards, and protect your brand at all costs.

We had not anticipated this turn of events in the negotiations. The government's insistence on the labor-quota linkage was highly unusual and unprecedented. Now we were dealing with a contingency with which we had no experience or preconceived game plan. But in the end, this unexpected turn of events proved monumental not only for Cambodia and its citizens but for the evolution of worldwide global trade relations.

Cham Prasidh came to the negotiations armed with the weight and authority of his position with the Cambodian government. But, more important, he came with the strength and character born of surviving unimaginable adversity. Prasidh was one of only 64 Cambodian intellectuals who had survived the Pol Pot killing fields. He was scheduled for extermination the day the country was liberated and as one of the few educated Cambodians to survive that country's holocaust, answered the call to government service as a way to help his nation recover from its dark past.

As we sat in our conference room in Washington, DC, I proceeded to detail all the reasons why Cambodia should not succumb to the U.S. government's demands. Not only was the proposal unorthodox and unprecedented, my position was that accepting it could potentially do great harm to Cambodia's reputation among the other nations that formed the Association of Southeast Asian Nations (ASEAN), a 10-country bloc formed to nurture economic growth and stability in the region. Furthermore, the restrictions would erode Cambodia's competitiveness and might cause some of its investors to seek opportunities elsewhere.

The minister listened carefully to my advice. Then, with an eloquence and passion born of his own experience and bolstered by sheer determination, he looked me in the eye and said, "Tom, I respect your advice but I am going to reject it. This linking of labor rights to trade benefits is good for the Cambodian people. It permits me to protect the Cambodian worker. My people have been through enough. They deserve the security of knowing their rights will be protected."

He even used an American expression. He called the U.S. government's proposal "a carrot and a stick." He knew that Cambodia's fledgling bureaucracy couldn't hope to enforce labor standards and regulations on its own. But with the support of the international community and the promised prize of additional quota, the same industrialists who would employ Cambodian laborers would now be required to also protect them. I accepted my client's logic and decision, but worked hard to improve the U.S. government's offer. In the end, we reached a compromise. Cambodia accepted the labor provisions and the U.S. government accepted our demands for higher quota.

I walked away from these negotiations understanding how important it is to expect the unexpected and, more important, to work within the frameworks given. I also came away with a deep understanding of the importance to maintain high ethical standards in all global dealings. As my doomsday prediction that industry would pull out of Cambodia proved to be unfounded, I also began to see that the fair labor requirements were actually being embraced by some companies, who understood that labor practices were linked to their corporate images in the minds of the increasingly knowledgeable and impressionable U.S. consumers. These were companies that would succeed in the changing world of global trade because they embraced the tenet: Protect your brand at all costs. By protecting their firm's reputation, they were indeed protecting their most valuable asset, their brand.

More than a decade has passed since these negotiations were concluded, and much has evolved with regard to international business transactions. Most notably, security has come to the forefront of all international business decisions. While cargo security and the safety of personnel traveling and living abroad has always been a critical concern for global traders, the terrorist attacks of September 11, 2001, have created new challenges for anyone moving goods across borders. In addition, advances in technology have made it easier to communicate sensitive information around the world and have created new offshore outsourcing opportunities that come with new problems in maintaining data security. For this reason I have added another universal Tenet of Global Trade: Stay secure in an insecure world.

I have expanded on the Tenets of Global Trade throughout the remainder of this book. Many of the lessons contained within these pages are based on my 30-year career as an international trade attorney and business advisor. Others stem from the business practices of corporations that have blazed trails in global trade, and some come from the missteps of companies that ran afoul of the tenets. Some, like the story of Cambodia's triumph, come from the histories of developing nations eager to participate in the global economy. All the tenets, however, were developed with one goal in mind: to assist entrepreneurs with finding a path to achieving prosperity on a global scale. My own personal journey in defining these principles began quite humbly.

IN THE BEGINNING

My career as an international trade attorney started quite by accident. In the fall of 1974, I was finishing up a federal judicial clerkship after receiving my law degree from Columbia University. My wife and I were expecting our first child and I knew that I needed to start thinking about how I was going to provide for my growing family. I decided to look for a position in international corporate law and, much to my surprise, ended up interviewing with a New York firm that specialized in an area of law that I had never heard of—customs and international trade. It is small wonder that becoming a customs and trade attorney had never crossed my mind. There were no courses in importing, exporting, or customs law offered at Columbia Law School and the topic wasn't tested on the Bar exam. At the time, there were fewer than 100 attorneys in the country actively practicing in this little-known field. The great import/export boom hadn't occurred yet and the term "globalization" had not made its way into the modern lexicon. Even though I was wholly unfamiliar with this specialized and unique area of law, it didn't take me long to come to the conclusion that the international trade field offered enormous potential.

Shortly after I joined that firm, Gilbert Lee Sandler came on board. Lee's background was with the Department of Justice where he litigated cases involving customs and trade. Here was a brilliant international trade attorney who had an abundance of trial experience, knew a great deal about customs law, and was admitted to practice before the customs court, which later became known as the Court of International Trade. Since both Lee and I were members of the Florida Bar, and there were no attorneys practicing our type of trade law in Miami at the time, making a move to South Florida to open our own practice began to look like a promising idea. Besides, there were no trade lawyers south of Washington, DC, or east of Los Angeles.

In the mid-1970s, businesspeople were keeping an eye on Latin America and the Caribbean. The Cuban diaspora that began in 1959 had sent a slew of businessmen experienced in freight forwarding and customs cargo clearance to the Miami area. These Havana-trained entrepreneurs were oriented toward Spanish-speaking countries and Miami was fast becoming a transportation hub for Latin America. Miami had everything—an international airport, a busy seaport, and rail and truck access to both. There was also an entrepreneurial determination permeating the area's business community, a pioneer spirit that would sweep South Florida into the forefront of the global trade stage.

The Miami-based law firm of Sandler & Travis, PA opened its doors on March 1, 1977. Lee and I kept a small office in New York while focusing the base of our operations in South Florida. Lee, a Miami native, had ample contacts in the community. We landed our first local client, an infant's clothing manufacturer, on that very afternoon. Fortunately, we were able to quickly resolve his problem and also obtain a sizable refund on customs duties that he did not expect. Following this victory, our reputation began to spread among the local *garmentos* and soon we became the go-to firm in South Florida for apparel issues. We also developed considerable expertise in transportation matters and outbound cargo. We came to understand the commercial importance of the Miami-based Cuban community, the regional importance of Latin America, and how the clothing industry was about to explode in Miami. A vast migration southward was taking place as U.S. apparel companies began to jettison their domestic operations and spread out across the Caribbean and Latin America. And we were there to guide these free-wheeling entrepreneurs as they took their first steps into the international arena.

Much of apparel production's steady migration southward occurred as a natural continuation of the trend that had begun after the Civil War. Historically, the apparel business has migrated south in search of lower labor costs. In the late nineteenth-century northeastern factories had relocated to the South to take advantage of a Reconstruction workforce; now, these same companies were setting their sights on developing nations south of the border. Spurred in large part by this trend, Miami was becoming the center of trade for Latin America, both outbound and inbound. This is an important point. Trading was definitely a two-way street. Congress had passed trade legislation—the "807 Program"—that allowed for a duty break on items that were assembled abroad from components fabricated in the United States. The apparel industry was out in full force exporting U.S. components to offshore factories and then importing the finished garments from these Third World operations. The vast increase in both imports from and exports to Latin America put South Florida on every global trader's map.

The late 1970s and early 1980s were an exciting time for international trade in South Florida. The global economy, the effect of these trade programs, and the pioneer spirit of the Miami trade entrepreneurs all came together in a unique and fortuitous way. It was a rough and tumble time for the local trade community. These were the *Miami Vice* days. And for the Sandler & Travis law firm, there was an accompanying geometric progression in our business expansion. The more business we got, the more we learned as we ran into every possible permutation of problems that could occur as a result of outsourcing and offshoring. By the 1980s we were representing importers and exporters in just about every industry under the sun. We were involved with food and agriculture, pharmaceuticals and chemicals, electronics and automotive goods. Our clients were importers, exporters, manufacturers, retailers, customs brokers, and freight forwarders.

Our firm was also expanding. In the early 1980s, Len Rosenberg and the late Ron Gerdes joined our ranks. Both were experienced government customs attorneys, and they were both instrumental in bringing our expertise to the next level as we embraced ever-more complex technical impediments to the free flow of goods across borders. By the early 1990s, the firm had become Sandler, Travis & Rosenberg, PA (ST&R) and we had added many new faces and opened offices around the country. In the late 1990s, we established a vibrant Government Relations and Trade Negotiations Group ably led by Ambassador Ron Sorini representing clients and governments as they sought to create more favorable environments through trade agreements and legislation. Today, we have international offices in Ottawa, Beijing, and Sao Paulo. We have ridden the wave of global expansion with our clients and our firm has flourished as they prospered.

Many of the clients we worked with in the western hemisphere became involved in Asian trade and production. The Chinese had experienced their own diaspora and Chinese businessmen were expanding their operations and influence throughout the world trade community. The Asian tigers were exporting in growing numbers and our client base began to expand into the Asia-Pacific region. Soon I was traveling to Asia on a regular basis and we beefed up our staff with top-notch Asian customs and trade professionals. Sandler, Travis & Rosenberg established a strong foothold in the region.

Early on, my partners and I formed Sandler & Travis Trade Advisory Services (STTAS) as an information resources and trade consulting sister company. With the addition of two of the trade community's more accomplished practitioners—Bob Schaffer, former assistant commissioner of customs, and Al D'Amico, a renowned customs broker and leader in the automotive trade—we were representing the world's largest automaker and a slew of automotive parts suppliers through our Detroit office and were intimately involved in Customs' modernization and border security initiatives. Our principals were sitting on government committees and participating in trade policy formulation.

Today, ST&R and STTAS clients include foreign countries seeking representation in their free trade negotiations with the United States, top multinational corporations, and a large and varied community of small and medium-size companies. Many of these companies are forging ahead to construct creative new business paradigms in the ever-changing global business landscape, and operating under the leadership of some of the world's most creative global thinkers. It is from these experiences that the following Tenets of Global Trade are derived.

TAKE ADVANTAGE OF TRADE AGREEMENTS: THINK OUTSIDE THE BORDER

Free trade agreements and trade preference programs provide global entrepreneurs with a clear competitive advantage. Decisions about where to set up a business venture, how to locate the best sourcing opportunities, and how to develop a strategic plan for the future are all dependent on a thorough knowledge of the trade opportunities these programs provide. New multicountry alliances are being formed all the time. Global entrepreneurs need to aggressively pursue their interests during trade agreement negotiations by defining a clear agenda and getting involved in the trade policy formulation process.

THE UNDERWEAR WAR

For the greater part of the twentieth century, Fruit of the Loom produced and sold more undergarments than any other company on the globe. But in the early 1990s, business began to change for this renowned sultan of skivvies—and not for the better. The situation in which Fruit of the Loom found itself may have had less to do with what the company did *wrong* than with what it failed to do *right*.

Simply put, the company delayed looking for opportunities outside of the U.S. border. This crucial decision left Fruit of the Loom vulnerable to the advances of another leading undergarment manufacturer. The company was Sara Lee Knit Products, now known as Hanesbrands, Inc.

Known for the popular Hanes underwear brand, Sara Lee was one of Fruit of the Loom's most aggressive competitors. With an eye on expanding market share and lowering production costs, company executives initiated a forceful campaign to explore business opportunities beyond U.S. borders.

That a major U.S. apparel producer would start exploring outside of U.S. borders for opportunities to lower costs was not surprising, given the apparel industry's history of production migration in search of lower labor costs. Toward the end of the twentieth century, forward-looking branded apparel companies were aggressively setting their sights on developing manufacturing capacity in nations south of the border.

Sara Lee was one of those companies. It made a decision to take advantage of a trade preference program that provided tariff benefits for imported goods as well as relief from quota (quantitative restrictions on U.S. imports). In a bold and strategic move, the company invested heavily in U.S. textile plants and moved a substantial amount of its sewing operations to the Caribbean Basin, where labor costs were markedly lower. Fruit of the Loom, on the other hand, kept the majority of its production in the

United States. By the mid-1990s, by implementing its off-shore sewing operations, Sara Lee/Hanes had become the new underwear leader. By the time the new millennium rolled around, Fruit of the Loom, for a multitude of reasons, had filed for bankruptcy. Although the company subsequently emerged from this condition (after being acquired by the Berkshire Hathaway Corporation), it has yet to recapture its prior market dominance.

TRADE PROGRAMS AS CHANGE AGENTS

Sara Lee won the underwear war partially through its ability to quickly shift its manufacturing practices in accordance with an advantageous trade program. Trade programs change the status quo. They foster competition, open up markets, and allow for the unencumbered flow of goods and services between countries and continents. Global businesses can reap significant benefits if they understand how these programs work and how they can interject themselves into the negotiations as they are being formed.

Trade programs fall into two categories: preference programs and free trade agreements (FTAs). Preference programs are unilaterally established by one country in favor of another country or group of countries, generally without demanding something in return. Preference programs are normally created to bolster the economies of developing countries. Free trade agreements, however, are bilateral or multilateral accords negotiated among nations for the benefit of all parties. While the fine print in each agreement specifies complex rules of eligibility for products and services, the general premise under which most

FTAs operate is the promotion of a freer flow of goods and services among participating nations.

Preferences and trade agreements have also been used as vehicles to quell insurgencies, promote capitalism and democracy, bring political adversaries together, and promote progressive labor and environmental standards. Importantly, they have also been used by aggressive companies to bolster their bottom lines and, in some cases, to foil competitors through the imposition of trade restrictions that affect competing goods.

Preferences Promote Economic Development and Stability

Current preference programs significantly impact U.S. imports. In 2005, the total value of imports under preference programs exceeded $104 billion.[1] While it would be impossible to describe each program in detail here, a few programs serve as solid examples of how preferences bolster a developing country's economy while enhancing business opportunities.

One of the early U.S. preference programs was the Generalized System of Preferences (GSP), first implemented on January 1, 1976, for a 10-year period. This program was designed to promote economic growth in the developing world by allowing eligible products grown or manufactured in developing nations to enter U.S. commerce free of duty. The U.S. GSP program has been renewed periodically since 1976, most recently in 2006, when President George W. Bush signed legislation authorizing the program to continue through 2008. Today the Office of the U.S. Trade Representative (USTR) reports that more than 4,650 products (from beef to sardines, pine nuts to pesticides) from 144 designated developing nations and territories can enter the United States duty-free under the program.

The African Growth and Opportunity Act (AGOA), first passed by Congress in 2000, is a preference program designed to create new commercial opportunities for people in sub-Saharan Africa. Two-way trade between the United States and sub-Saharan African countries has increased 115 percent since the program's launch. In 2005, total U.S. exports to the region rose to $10.3 billion and included agricultural goods, machinery, and transportation equipment. Total U.S. imports from the region reached $50.3 billion, with 98 percent of these imports entering the United States duty-free. Although the vast majority of imports from AGOA countries continue to consist of petroleum products, other goods that have seen increases in exports to the United States under the program include apparel, chemicals, agricultural products, diamonds, and cocoa.[2]

The Andean Trade Promotion and Drug Eradication Act (ATPDEA) offers economic incentives to combat drug production and trafficking in Bolivia, Colombia, Ecuador, and Peru. Enacted as part of the Trade Act of 2002, the ATPDEA expanded the 1991 Andean Trade Preference Act (ATPA) by offering trade benefits to help Andean countries develop and strengthen legitimate industries. It provides duty-free access to U.S. markets for approximately 5,600 products from these countries.[3]

Free Trade as a Two (or More)-Way Street

As of January 2007, the United States had signed on to 12 free trade agreements, all formed within the past 25 years. Some agreements are regional and multilateral, such as the North American Free Trade Agreement (NAFTA), which promotes open trade between the United States, Canada, and Mexico, and the U.S.-Dominican Republic-Central America Free Trade Agreement (US-DR-CAFTA), which promotes trade between the United States, the Dominican Republic, El Salvador, Nicaragua, Honduras, Guatemala, and Costa Rica. Others are bilateral, such as the FTAs with Israel, Jordan, Chile, Australia, Singapore, Morocco, Bahrain, and Oman. Colombia, Peru, and Panama have signed agreements with the United States but await action by the U.S. Congress.

As this book heads to the publisher, the United States is actively in negotiations with Korea and Malaysia with hopes to conclude them in early 2007. Free trade agreement talks have also been held with Thailand, the United Arab Emirates, and the Southern African Customs Union (consisting of South Africa, Botswana, Lesotho, Namibia, and Swaziland). Behind the scenes, businesses and politicians all over the world are opening dialogues on even more agreements.

These change agents we call preference programs and free trade agreements are so profound in their impact that regions across the globe have jumped on the bandwagon. Europe has them. Asian countries have banded together to create free trade areas. Much of Latin America has joined forces for the free flow of trade.

As borders are obliterated, trade export opportunities open up for domestic manufacturers who find new markets to peddle their wares. According to the USTR, in the first year of the U.S.-Singapore FTA, America's trade surplus with Singapore tripled. During the first three months after implementation of the U.S.-Australia FTA, America's trade surplus with the Aussies grew by almost 32 percent.[4]

MAKING THE SYSTEM WORK FOR YOU

Not all preferences and trade agreements benefit all industries equally. Trade programs are formed through a complex and sometimes chaotic process of aggressive lobbying, government agenda setting, and industry manipulation. Powerful domestic interests can delay or quash a beneficial program and it is often incumbent on industry to jump into the process to ensure that its interests are being addressed.

The program used to such great advantage by Sara Lee/Hanes was the Special Access Program, a trade preference that was established through the efforts of a small consortium of well-known branded apparel producers. What makes the story of the Special Access Program so compelling is that the program on which it is based—the Caribbean Basin Initiative—specifically excluded textile and apparel from the program's parameters. But Sara Lee and like-minded apparel producers refused to sit back and allow the powerful domestic textiles lobby to bar them from a trade program that afforded other industries substantial benefits. It took the solidarity of like-minded entrepreneurs—some of whom were aggressive competitors—and a willingness to compromise to win significant trade benefits.

Creating Consortiums: How the Dominican Republic Became the Isle of Dockers

In 1983, the Reagan administration and its policymakers were concerned about events in Central America. This was the era of the Sandinista regime in Nicaragua, and the opposition Contras (referred to as "freedom fighters" by President Reagan) had established an insurgency against the leftist Sandinistas. The Berlin Wall would not fall for another six years and the Cold War was still very much defining U.S. foreign policy. The White House looked on the potential spread of Communism in the western hemisphere as perhaps America's greatest threat. In response, the Caribbean Basin Initiative (CBI) was created as one avenue to fight Communism in the Caribbean Basin and Central America.

The CBI was designed to spur economic activity in Central America and the Caribbean Basin by providing additional duty-free access to the United States for regionally produced goods. The thought was that if impoverished nations became full participants in a capitalist society, democratic values spurred on by a freer market economy would follow. Under the provisions of the CBI, as long as designated manufactured goods contained the statutory level of local content (35 percent) and met certain other requirements, the imported goods could enter the U.S. stream of commerce with few restrictions.

While the initiative provided significant and immediate benefits to industries employing light assembly and processing operations, including makers of hardware, lighting, and auto parts, and specialty goods such as fishing rods and reels, the CBI did not contain a provision benefiting apparel products. Ironically, apparel production was the industry most likely to further the CBI's goals of spurring economic development and employment in the region because of the ease with which it can be established and operated. But because apparel manufacturers were left out of the CBI, clothing imports from the Caribbean remained subject to high duty rates and quantitative restrictions under a strict quota program.

Unwilling to succumb to what they perceived as unfair trade discrimination, a number of leaders in the branded apparel industry, including VF Corporation, Haggar Clothing Corporation, Sara Lee, and Levi Strauss & Co., began looking for ways they could increase their presence in the region while reaping trade benefits in parity with other industries. At the time, there were no trade associations these forward-thinking companies could turn to for support in their efforts to gain inclusion in the CBI program. The traditional fiber, yarn, fabric, and apparel associations all had strong protectionist bents, so these branded apparel producers decided to band together to find a way to get their interests heard by the politicians setting trade policy.

Offshore Assembly

Levi Strauss & Co. was particularly keen to move some of its operations offshore. Lower labor costs, while certainly a draw, were not the only reason the company was looking to the Caribbean Basin and Mexico at that time. It also needed to increase its production capacity. In a move that would go down in the annals of fashion industry history as a stroke of design and marketing genius, Levi had reworked the chinos style of casual trousers and created what would become one of its most popular brands, Dockers®. But the success of the new line depended on finding a way to fill the mammoth orders for the new product. The company's self-owned U.S. factories were already running at full volume with its blue jeans manufacturing business and it needed new facilities to produce the new brand, so Levi geared up for a move to the Caribbean Basin. The company wanted to take advantage of the same duty-savings opportunities that importers of other products were realizing under CBI, and proposed that it be afforded the partial duty benefits of the long-established "807" program.

Under the 807 preference program (renamed "9802" under the Harmonized Tariff Schedule) manufacturers prepare component parts in the United States, then bundle together the ready-for-assembly items and ship them to offshore facilities where they are confected into completed goods and sent back to the United States. The 807 program allows companies to take advantage of the cheaper labor costs in developing countries and realize significant cost savings in the form of lower duties on the imported goods. Importers pay duty on the value of the assembly operations plus some transportation costs, rather than the value of the garments themselves. As a result, a $10 pair of men's trousers that would normally have duty costs of $1.70 could be imported under the 807 program with a duty cost of only $0.34—an 80 percent savings. The only glitch for Levi was the textile and apparel quota—quantitative restrictions on how many garments could be imported into the United States from a particular country.

Controlled by the complex Multifiber Arrangement, a now-defunct international agreement under which signatory countries could apply quantitative restrictions on apparel and textile imports to protect domestic industry, the majority of quota earmarked for the production of pants in Mexico and most of the Caribbean countries was already being utilized and chances were remote that more would be allocated. And moving production to Asia wasn't an option due to the prohibitive costs involved with obtaining the rights to export garments. These quota costs, coupled with increases in transportation and other logistical expenses, would have killed the program.

By remaining in the western hemisphere and overseeing operations close to the border, Levi could utilize efficiency in its supply chain and manufacturing expertise. So Levi found itself in a predicament. It could manufacture its Dockers in new offshore facilities south of the border and take advantage of reduced production costs and retain control over the supply chain and quality of production but, because of the quantitative restrictions on how many trousers could be exported to the United States, the company would not be able to get them into the country.

Levi, along with several other apparel companies, approached Sandler, Travis & Rosenberg (ST&R) to assist with this dilemma. The powerful domestic textile and apparel trade association lobbyists were fighting attempts to make it easier for U.S. companies to manufacture offshore.

The solution?

Sandler, Travis & Rosenberg formed a trade association on behalf of Levi and like-minded apparel companies, the U.S. Apparel Industry Council (USAIC), and set out to lobby for the inclusion of apparel in the CBI preferences.

The USAIC had some early success with convincing the Reagan administration for quota-free entry of apparel from the region, but hit a wall when the idea was floated around Capitol Hill. The U.S. fabric lobby opposed any new quota-free programs that allowed foreign fabric to be used in the manufacture of the garments. After a great deal of negotiating and maneuvering, the parties agreed to a new program for the region that allowed garments whose components had been cut to shape exclusively *from U.S. fabric* to be exported to the Caribbean or Mexico for sewing and reimported as finished garments quota-free. Because it included a requirement that the fabric be made in U.S. mills, this compromise pacified most of the U.S. textiles industry. By compromising to make use of domestic fabric a criterion for program eligibility, USAIC and its supporters were able to seal the deal to their advantage.

Like the 807 program, duty was assessed only on the labor costs involved in completing the garments. That program—dubbed Special Access for the Caribbean and Special Regime for Mexico—was established in 1986 and resulted in an explosion in apparel trade in the region. The value of imports of cotton trousers from the Caribbean hit almost $300 million in 1986, the first year of the program, up 600 percent from 1984 levels. The Dominican Republic became the "Isle of Dockers" and Mexico became the blue jeans capital of the world. The western hemisphere became the center of this production and by 1999 more than 50 percent of all U.S. imports of trousers came from the region.

The textile and apparel CBI saga is a dramatic example of how industry can play a major role in creating trade policy. By refusing to sit idly by and watch other industries prosper through a new trade program, the apparel industry stood up and made sure it got a seat at the CBI table for itself and its customers.

Peace Through Prosperity: The U.S.-Israel-Jordan Qualifying Industrial Zones

Sometimes trade opportunities are already in existence, and it takes a forward-thinking entrepreneur to tap into those opportunities. Such was the case with an experimental trade program designed to turn adversaries into business partners and enemies into allies, albeit cautious ones.

This is precisely what happened between the Israelis and the Jordanians in the late 1990s and, more recently, became possible with Israeli-Egyptian relations as well. In 1996, the U.S. Congress decided to examine the Israeli-Arab conflict from an economic perspective. Could peace be encouraged through trade? Would prosperity pave the road to greater cooperation between Arabs and Jews?

Congress authorized the president to allow Jordan, Egypt, and even the Palestinian territories to reap substantial benefits under the U.S.-Israel FTA through the creation of joint ventures between Israeli businesses and their

Arab counterparts. Formed in 1985, the U.S.-Israel FTA was the first free trade agreement the United States entered into. Under that agreement, trade between the United States and Israel is duty-free as long as the products being sold across borders originate in either or both countries. In the past 20 years of the accord, both Israel and the United States have enjoyed healthy benefits. In 2005, shipments from the United States to Israel were valued at nearly $10 billion. Israeli exports to the United States that year totaled almost $17 billion, up 663 percent since 1985. Israel is now America's eighteenth biggest trading partner.[5]

That the United States would partner with a strategic democratic ally in the volatile Middle East is hardly a surprise. But the offshoots of the U.S.-Israel FTA programs encouraging greater economic cooperation between Israel and its Arab neighbors (and even the Palestinians) are more unusual in the trade arena.

Under the 1996 accord, Jordan, Egypt, and the Palestinian territories (the West Bank and Gaza Strip) were invited to designate certain industrial parks and facilities as Qualifying Industrial Zones (QIZ). An article manufactured in a QIZ (pronounced "quiz") can gain duty-free access to the United States as long as it is considered to be a "product" of a QIZ and at least 35 percent of its value is represented by materials and/or direct costs of processing attributable to either Israel or the QIZ. The upshot of the legislation is that goods produced in Jordanian or Egyptian QIZs from Israeli inputs are afforded the same beneficial trade rules as goods manufactured entirely in Israel. In essence, the QIZ program is, by design, a mechanism to foster trade relations between Israel and its Arab neighbors. (Given present circumstances, there are no current plans for Palestinian territory participation.)

From the outset, the QIZ idea had its skeptics. Almost everyone in the trade community, and more than a few involved in Middle East policy, scoffed at the notion that promoting cooperation between Arab and Israeli business could produce anything close to a peace dividend, let alone be an impetus for profitable business ventures. Of course, like any new business paradigm, the key to working with a trade program like QIZ is to understand how it works and seize opportunities quickly and with strategic foresight. Omar Salah, then a 28-year-old Jordanian entrepreneur, did just that.

One Man's Vision: QIZs and the Peace Dividend

Given the history of the region and the ongoing animosity between the parties, it is no surprise that the unique trading opportunities under the QIZ program were not instantly embraced in the beneficiary countries. Egypt did not authorize its first QIZ until 2004. Even Jordan, arguably another close ally of the United States, waited three years to make its QIZ program operational. The first Jordanian QIZ opened its doors in 1999, largely due to the foresight and drive of Salah, a visionary who started laying the groundwork for Jordanian business opportunities with Israelis as soon as the ink was dry on the 1994 Jordan-Israel peace treaty.

Salah immediately grasped the potential benefits of the QIZ scenario. Unfettered access to U.S. markets could spark a much-needed industrial revolution within Jordan that could bolster the country's economy and empower its citizenry. The QIZ program could also provide untold opportunities to the two million Palestinians who had made Jordan their home.

To find partners for a new venture, Salah would have to travel to Israel—no small feat for a Jordanian national in the mid-1990s. Jordanians weren't exactly welcomed into Israel and, of course, Israelis were not regularly traveling to Jordan for business. Nevertheless, fortified with a strong entrepreneurial spirit and a willingness to think outside the regional political box, Salah trekked to Tel Aviv with one goal in mind—to seek out Israeli entrepreneurs who had the foresight and economic motivation to partner with their Arab neighbors in Jordan. Salah began cold-calling Israeli apparel companies. What Salah was offering, under the auspices of the QIZ program, was utilization of less costly Jordanian labor combined with duty-free access to the United States and, in the case of apparel, quota-free access as well.

Israeli businessman Dov Lautman and his company Delta Galil decided to take a chance on this young Arab entrepreneur. Together, Salah and Lautman formed Century Wear, a knitted garment joint venture. Lautman contributed his company's apparel expertise, design know-how, and access to export markets. Salah brought production management and manufacturing proficiency. The joint Israeli-Jordanian venture created more than 850 new jobs in Jordan with salary rates exceeding similar Jordanian payrolls by 40 percent. Sales topped $10 million in the first year of operation. The vast benefits of the program soon caught the attention of major branded apparel companies in the United States. One in particular, J.C. Penney, under the vision and leadership of key sourcing executive Peter McGrath, committed a significant portion of its orders to the Jordanian QIZs. Other Jordanian entrepreneurs followed suit, forming additional QIZ parks;

by 2002, more than 30,000 Jordanians were employed in QIZs and exports topped $400 million.[6]

The program, of course, was not without its detractors. Century Investment Group, Salah's Jordanian holding company, was blacklisted by the Anti-Normalisation Committee, a Jordanian group dedicated to ending all links with Israel. And some Palestinians and Jordanians looked at employment in a cooperative venture with Israel as nothing short of treason. One such QIZ critic was, at the time, a high-ranking Hamas official who found out that his daughter had taken a position in a factory in the Irbid Zone, a QIZ industrial park founded by Salah. The official immediately ordered his daughter to quit her job, incensed that she would be cooperating with the Israelis. But the young woman convinced her father to visit the factory, to see for himself how the workers were treated, how the salaries were more than competitive, and how women were being empowered through economic opportunities that afforded them a decent wage and relative autonomy. The Hamas leader took his daughter up on her invitation and, after surveying the Irbid Zone and talking to the workers, acquiesced to his daughter's wishes. He allowed her to continue her employment and even admitted that the economic stability the QIZ factories brought to the region was beneficial to the Palestinian workers employed there and especially to the women, many of whom were able, for the first time, to make significant contributions to the maintenance of their households and families.

Egypt Finally Implements QIZ

The Egyptian textiles industry received a wake-up call in 2004. Worldwide quota on textile and apparel exports was scheduled to be abolished in 2005 and industry leaders were up in arms about the potential repercussions to the vibrant Egyptian textile trade. Conventional wisdom was that China, with its stronghold in the apparel export markets, would essentially take over global apparel production once quotas no longer restricted the behemoth producer's access to foreign markets. But even with quota abolished, tariffs on textile and apparel goods remained high. Egyptian producers understood that adopting QIZ operations in their country would give them a great advantage—tariff-free access to the mammoth U.S. apparel market. Additionally, Egyptian entrepreneurs had watched closely Jordan's success under the QIZ and were hungry to follow in Jordan's footsteps and eventually construct a full free trade agreement with the United States. Even though the implementation of Egypt's QIZ program had been stalled for political reasons for 10 years, industry pressure prevailed, and in 2005 Egypt opened its first designated QIZ.

By all accounts, the implementation of the QIZ program in Egypt has achieved great success. Egypt's garment industry was already quite sophisticated. Unlike Jordan, whose apparel production industry was, at that time, still at the ground floor level as far as the skills and experience of its workforce, Egypt could offer customers the economic benefits of long-standing, sophisticated, vertically-integrated operations that could handle everything from fabric creation to garment completion. The Israeli press reports that due to the QIZ program, by the end of 2005 Egypt had increased its trade with Israel by 130 percent and created an estimated 15,000 new jobs, a figure that rose to 30,000 by the end of 2006.[7]

While 79 percent of the 606 companies designated under the Egyptian QIZ program are textile related, other industries such as footwear, building materials, machinery, plastics, and prepared foods have also benefited. The Egyptian Ministry of Trade and Industry touts the ultimate goal of the QIZ program by saying, "While this protocol is a non-reciprocal arrangement between Egypt and the United States, it is expected to be a step towards a Free Trade Agreement (FTA) between the two countries."[8]

From QIZ to FTA—The U.S.-Jordan Free Trade Evolution

One of the clear goals of trade initiatives is to integrate markets, spur demand, and increase opportunities for all concerned. The success of the Jordanian QIZ program not only spurred Egypt to ratify the QIZ program but also was the impetus for a separate free trade agreement between Jordan and the United States. Jordan's King Abdullah asked the United States to enter into an FTA with Jordan, emphasizing the kingdom's close relationship with the United States and its role in helping to bring stability to the region. King Abdullah recognized that the success of the QIZ program, particularly in the textiles trade, could be expanded to other industries if the QIZ restrictions were lifted and Jordanian business was allowed to work directly with U.S. business interests.

For the most part, navigating a free trade agreement through myriad political land mines can be a staggering proposition. Each industry that might be affected wants to put its own fingerprint on the agreement, and the lobbying and posturing and stalling tactics used by industry advocates can delay or even kill a proposed accord. This is the primary reason why every president since 1974— both Democrats and Republicans—has sought and received Trade Promotion Authority (TPA), also called "fast track" authority, to push trade legislation through Congress. Under TPA, whole agreements proposed by the administration are given a full up or down vote; there are no amendments or dissecting of what is presented for approval so obstructionists in Congress or particular constituencies can't derail otherwise sensible political and commercial opportunities. Even though the Republican-controlled Congress had not granted President Clinton TPA during the U.S.-Jordan FTA process, the agreement easily sailed through Congress. While the president and Congress were deeply divided on many issues, the obvious benefits of rewarding an important ally like Jordan and making a statement as to the importance of economic integration prevailed. The agreement was signed into law on September 28, 2001.

Today, we see that the success of the QIZ program and the subsequent U.S.-Jordan FTA has provided a model of free trade for the Arab world. In recent years, the United States has entered into FTAs with Morocco, Oman, and Bahrain and is in the final stages of discussions with the United Arab Emirates. Many international business interests hold out hope that the Palestinian territories could one day opt for peace through prosperity by implementing the QIZ program.

Free trade agreements and preference programs, whether designed to assist developing nations, promote peace, or consolidate the interests of regional allies, are an important weapon in the global trader's arsenal. Understanding and applying their benefits to your business systems is an important element to becoming a player on the international stage.

Tenets of Global Trade

1. *Familiarize yourself with preference programs and trade agreements.* The global trader must understand the

significance of trade accords in forming strategic business plans. Key decisions such as where to source products, how open a market is for exports, and whether services can be freely offered in another country are dependent, in large part, on the trade agreements and preferences that are established with a particular country or geographic region. Even the most powerful industry leader can end up falling behind from a failure to read the global landscape and adjust operations accordingly. Keep up with what is going on in international trade in your industry. Subscribe to information services such as ST&R's *WorldTrade\ INTERACTIVE*, the Bureau of National Affairs' *International Trade Daily*, and Inside Washington Publishers' *Inside U.S. Trade*, and monitor relevant government websites like those of the U.S. Trade Representative (www.ustr.gov) and the U.S. Department of Commerce (www.commerce.gov).

2. *Read the fine print.* Understand fully the preferences and FTAs that affect your products and services and isolate the pros and cons in the regions where you plan to conduct business. Decipher the details, mine the minutiae, and use this information to formulate a sound strategic plan for your particular operation and goals.

3. *Participate in the process.* Define a clear agenda and get involved in the international trade policy formulation process. Become active in trade associations that promote your business goals, and if such an association doesn't exist, find like-minded industrialists (some of whom will likely be your competi-

tors) and form your own organization. If you don't have a legislative tracking arm in your company or in-house government relations professionals, seek out consultants who understand your industry and issues. Not all lobbying firms, even those who profess to have an inside track on trade issues, have expertise in every industry. Be sure that the expert advice you are paying for is the best that money can buy.

4. *Seize opportunities when they arise.* Often the winners in global trade are those who are the first out of the starting gate. By becoming a trailblazer, you will not only beat out the competition, you will also play a major role in defining the terms of engagement.

3

PROTECT YOUR BRAND AT ALL COSTS

While safeguarding intellectual property rights is the cornerstone of brand protection, international business must also focus on becoming a respected global citizen. It is imperative that you take affirmative steps to preserve not only your patents, copyrighted materials, and trademarks, but also your international reputation by paying attention to the labor and environmental practices of offshore facilities with which you do business. Protecting your brand means protecting your company's image by taking steps to ensure that it is not soured by unsavory partners who engage in labor rights violations or lax environmental practices.

PROTECT YOUR BRAND

In May 2003, the Norwegian Church Aid (NCA), a Christian human rights group in Norway, charged Tommy Hilfiger with human rights abuses in connection with its alleged use of a factory located in the northern Thailand province of Mae Sot. According to NCA, the factory in question employed Burmese workers who were underpaid, overworked, and housed in deplorable conditions. Many of these workers were young women who, according to the Norwegian press, were made to churn out Tommy Hilfiger branded garments at breakneck speed. Tommy Hilfiger was taken to task by the international press for its sourcing transgressions. The only problem was Tommy Hilfiger wasn't working with this factory. For six short months in 1999, Tommy Hilfiger had contracted with the factory under investigation but pulled its business a full four years before the inquiry and allegations arose. It turned out that at the time the allegations of abhorrent labor practices were made, the factory was producing counterfeit Tommy Hilfiger goods. The company found itself in the surreal position of having to defend itself against allegations of abuse by a factory that was stealing its trademark. Tommy Hilfiger pushed back with a full-impact public relations campaign, but not before its reputation had been smeared and its brand bruised.

You Are Your Brand

Your company, your products and services, and your brand are inseparable. As you move into the global arena, new safeguards must be employed if you are to avoid compromising your company's greatest asset—its reputation. This means that you must learn how to protect your intellectual property—including copyrights, trademarks, and patents—as well as preserve your company's good name.

The illegal production of counterfeit and substandard goods not only dilutes a brand's image and cheapens its appeal, but can result in catastrophic consequences, as in the case of sometimes ineffective or even dangerous counterfeit pharmaceuticals. Counterfeiting conspiracies account for astronomical losses to companies around the world.

Nothing can send a company's brand south faster than allegations of labor improprieties or environmental missteps. And because the best defense is a good offense, addressing these brand-sensitive concerns *before* you set your sights on offshoring can mean the difference between global trade success and failure.

While governments attempt to enact safeguards to protect intellectual property, balance the interests of business and workers, and protect the environment, ultimately, it is up to each enterprise to ensure that its brand is protected.

The Worldwide Counterfeiting Crisis

Businesses operating abroad must understand how to protect their intellectual property on a global scale. According to the International Chamber of Commerce, as much as 7 percent of world trade is in counterfeit goods, costing industry around $650 billion a year.[1] Organized crime syndicates and terrorist groups, including al Qaeda, fund their operations through sales of counterfeit goods.

At one point, perhaps, knockoffs could have been considered a problem primarily for high-end apparel and accessories. Anyone who has walked the streets of any city in the world knows how easy it is to find vendors hawking everything from fake Louis Vuitton bags and rogue "Rolex" watches to rip-off "designer" jeans and cheaply made athletic shoes sporting logos from name-brand styles. Today, however, the problem is infinitely more widespread. If a product has any sort of significant market, chances are someone is making a fake version and raking in a lot of money selling it. Media reports are full of instances of raids of everything from phony Hewlett-Packard inkjet cartridges in Brazil to bogus Nokia cell phone parts in France to counterfeit computer chips in China. It's not hard to see why so many criminals are getting into this business—start-up costs are relatively low, profit margins are high, chances for getting caught are slim, and penalties for those who are apprehended are generally negligible.[2]

Counterfeiting is now everyone's problem, not only because of how far-reaching it has become but because many times it is virtually impossible to distinguish a genuine product from a phony. Crooks no longer slap together a cheap shirt or pair of pants and slap a shoddy name-brand label on it, seeking to pass it off to unsuspecting tourists. Technological advances have enabled counterfeiters to significantly increase the quality of the fakes they produce. The fit, finish, and operation of these forgeries can be nearly identical to the originals, at least for a while. But once the sham is discovered, it's your company's reputation that's going to take the hit.

Getting nailed for inferior goods is bad enough—in an instant it can destroy business relationships you have carefully cultivated for years and a public image built on otherwise responsible policies and actions. Even worse, however, is when a fake product with your name or logo on it results in death or injury to consumers. The sheer breadth of the counterfeiting problem in today's world means that there is an increasing chance that knockoff goods are making their way into uses where low quality can quickly translate into catastrophe. Products like drugs, baby formula, brake pads, and even airplane parts are being cheaply duplicated, and the results can be deadly. In

1989, a Norwegian jetliner crashed, killing 55 people. Among the reasons for the crash was the use of counterfeit fasteners.[3] In 2004, dozens of children died in China after being fed infant formula that contained virtually none of the nutrients the food product normally contains.[4] Experts have expressed growing concerns about the threat to public safety caused by bogus automobile and airplane parts.

Fake drugs pose a particular threat. The World Health Organization (WHO) estimates that 10 percent of the medicine on the global market is fake and that 25 percent of drugs in developing countries are counterfeit.[5] With the Internet providing an easy avenue for duping customers around the world, it is next to impossible to distinguish legitimate drugs from their sinister and often dangerous counterfeit counterparts. In 2003, Pfizer recalled 16.5 million tablets of Lipitor after a consumer tip resulted in a discovery that a fake version of the anti-cholesterol drug was being widely distributed across the United States.[6] Millions of fake Viagra pills are sold online every week. The Chinese government reported that 192,000 of its citizens died in 2001 due to counterfeit drugs.[7] According to WHO, almost any popular drug is routinely counterfeited and sold around the world, from "lifestyle medicines" such as hormones and steroids to treatments for diseases like malaria, AIDS, and cancer.[8]

International Enforcement Initiatives

The international community has long been up in arms about pervasive pirating and counterfeiting, but enforcement efforts have accelerated in recent years. One particularly notable advancement was the explicit linkage of intellectual property rights to trade in the Agreement on Trade-Related Aspects of Intellectual Property Rights

(TRIPS), part of the Uruguay Round negotiations that ultimately created the World Trade Organization (WTO) in 1995. Signing on to the agreement, which took effect in 1995, is a prerequisite to membership in WTO. TRIPS requires that WTO member countries apply uniform international trade principles with respect to intellectual property. It establishes minimum standards for the availability, scope, and use of intellectual property protection and spells out limitations and exceptions intended to balance intellectual property concerns with public health and economic development concerns. Least-developed countries were given until 2006 to adopt TRIPS' protective intellectual property rights (IPR) standards, with added time afforded for the implementation of these standards as they related to pharmaceuticals.

The U.S. Fight to Control Counterfeiting

With the scope of counterfeiting so broad and the dangers to business and society so real, protecting intellectual property has become one of the biggest commercial concerns for U.S. industry and the federal government. In October 2004, the Bush administration rolled out a major new intellectual property rights initiative that has become the framework for all government IPR protection efforts. The Strategy Targeting Organized Piracy (STOP!), a joint partnership between the Office of the U.S. Trade Representative; the Food and Drug Administration; and the departments of Commerce, Justice, Homeland Security, and State, encompasses a wide range of efforts, both domestically and internationally, to try and bring the problem under control. Government agencies are tasked with using risk management techniques and post-entry audits, as well as technologies and procedures originally developed to increase supply chain security (like the advance manifest rules for inbound cargo) to identify traffickers in fake goods. Companies are encouraged to take antipiracy measures throughout their supply chains, including making their own seizures where allowed by federal law. And the White House committed to increasing cooperation with foreign countries and multilateral organizations to share information, conduct joint enforcement efforts, and promote tougher rules.[9]

The government has also restructured itself to more actively promote intellectual property rights, including making it easier for businesses to get protection and stepping up efforts to nab violators. The Department of Commerce created a new position, coordinator for international intellectual property enforcement, which serves as the lead office for integrating efforts among U.S. agencies and conducting outreach to industry groups and foreign governments. The Office of the U.S. Trade Representative established a new Office of Intellectual Property and Innovation and a new assistant U.S. Trade Representative position to oversee it, and also named a chief negotiator for intellectual property enforcement. Intellectual property rights experts from Commerce, USTR, and the Department of Justice have been deployed overseas in places like Brazil, China, India, Russia, Thailand, and Egypt to provide better on-the-ground assistance for U.S. companies and enhance efforts to track down criminals.

In the context of international trade, the USTR often takes the lead, employing both bilateral and multilateral mechanisms to control IPR violations and protect U.S. interests abroad. Its annual "Special 301" report evaluates IPR protection and enforcement efforts in nearly 100 countries and employs a three-tiered system for ranking countries where problems have been identified. Placement on the Special 301 Watch List, the lowest level, serves as a wake-up call to countries falling short of their IP protection obligations. The list, which effectively warns those thinking about investing in the identified countries that their IP rights are likely not to be protected, is a powerful weapon in the U.S. government's arsenal in fighting piracy. Merely being named on the list can serve as an incentive for a country to clean up its IP enforcement act. If not, a country may be moved up to the Priority Watch List, which signals that the United States is extremely concerned about IPR violations, or designated as a Priority Foreign Country, which could ultimately lead to trade sanctions.

When being publicly called out fails to prompt improvements, the USTR can turn to other options. Virtually all U.S. trade preference programs include respect for intellectual property rights among their eligibility criteria, and threatening sanctions such as removal from the benefits of these programs can be extremely effective. The loss of the U.S. tariff benefits afforded under programs such as the Generalized System of Preferences or the Caribbean Basin Initiative has led to reform efforts in beneficiary developing nations.

Another favorite tool of USTR is placing IPR provisions in free trade agreements. Free trade agreements typically include commitments that are stronger and deeper than those in place under TRIPS or other international agreements. More important, these obligations are enforceable—the partner country can't just pay lip service to the idea and say it will try and do better. To go along with the stick of enforcement, the USTR offers the carrot of technical assistance; cooperating with foreign officials to draft stronger IP laws, strengthen enforcement capabilities, and train prosecutors and judges in IPR-specific issues.

The U.S. government considers protecting American ingenuity abroad a high priority. According to USTR Susan Schwab, "Americans are among the world's greatest innovators, in no small part because of the strength of our respect for intellectual property rights in the United States. In the global economy, maintaining protections for American innovations abroad is critical to advancing U.S. competitiveness. Protection of Intellectual Property by other nations is also critical to their own economic development, including promotion of indigenous innovations, creativity and access to innovations by consumers and promoters of innovation."[10]

Protecting Your Own Intellectual Property

While the government's efforts toward worldwide IP protection, as well as the advent of TRIPS and other international treaties, are increasing industry awareness and government enforcement of intellectual property rights, the problem is so widespread and pervasive that, as a practical matter, the onus is on the entrepreneur to protect his IP to the best of his ability.

The first line of defense in the international intellectual property wars is to examine your business and catalog your intellectual property and then decide what should be protected where. Once you have a handle on what you own and what it is worth, work with professionals to protect your intellectual property in the United States and abroad.

How and whether to register your intellectual property abroad depends on a number of factors: your present and future plans to conduct business outside the United States (innovative entrepreneurs in countries such as China are registering domain and brand names of U.S. companies, then selling them back to the rightful owner at exorbitant prices; it is in your best interest to beat them to the punch); the likelihood of your product being copied abroad; whether and to what extent foreign export markets or sourcing locations have signed patent or trademark agreements with the United States; whether a particular country or jurisdiction will permit third parties to register your trademark without any use requirement either before or after application; and the cost of applying for and maintaining the desired intellectual property protection relative to its value to your business, to name a few. If you decide to seek protection in multiple countries, see if you can take advantage of the Patent Cooperation Treaty or the Madrid Protocol, which allow companies to file one application with their national authorities to protect their patents and trademarks, respectively, in all participating countries.

Next, you will need to build an intellectual property protection strategy into your operating protocols. Be mindful of who you choose as business partners abroad and how much access they will have to your intellectual property. Conduct due diligence of potential and current foreign partners. Obtain an International Company Profile Report from the U.S. Commercial Service and if you determine that working with a particular foreign partner is desirable, work with an intellectual property professional to make sure that contract and subcontract language spells out who can use and/or register your property when and what happens to your branded products afterward.

Record your U.S.-registered trademarks and copyrights with U.S. Customs and Border Protection (CBP). Under its recordation program, CBP collects information from an intellectual property owner about specific registered trademarks, copyrights, or trade names, and then enters the information into an electronic database accessible by CBP officers across the country. Customs and Border Protection officials at U.S. ports actively monitor import and export shipments and will immediately seize counterfeit goods and detain those which bear "confusingly similar" trademarks. The agency has boosted its attention to this issue in recent years—more than 14,000 seizures of goods valued at over $155 million were made in fiscal year 2006, up from 3,244 seizures valued at $45.3 million in 2000.[11]

An ounce of prevention is worth a pound of cure, so the saying goes, and so taking preemptive steps like these to ensure that your IPR is guarded by the strongest possible protections before you jump into the global marketplace is a wise investment. But as Tommy Hilfiger knows all too well, even a company's best efforts to prevent counterfeiting, piracy, and other violations can fall short. That's when you have to be ready to pursue enforcement—an option that's increasingly feasible. In the United States, for example, importers who suspect that their intellectual property has been misappropriated can seek a Section 337 investigation by the U.S. International Trade Commission (ITC). Section 337 investigations (conducted pursuant to federal statute: 19 U.S.C. §1337) are designed to protect the interests of U.S. domestic industry against infringement of patents, trademarks, and copyrights; illegal use of trade secrets; and false advertising. To remedy such actions, the ITC can issue orders prohibiting the entry of infringing goods or directing violators to halt acts that constitute unfair competition. Monetary damages, however, are not available under this remedy and 337 actions can be quite costly. If you believe that your intellectual property is being violated or you are being affected by other unfair competition practices, contact the ITC's Office of Unfair Import Investigations.

There is always the option of resorting to private litigation to stop an infringer from interfering with your business. This tactic, while sometimes necessary and frequently effective, can also be costly and is more time consuming than a Section 337 action. It is always better to take a proactive stance to protect your interests first, rather than relying on reactive practices such as litigation to remedy a situation that is likely already out of control.

LABOR AND IMAGE: PROTECTING YOUR BRAND

As the Tommy Hilfiger story also reveals, allegations of unfair and exploitative labor practices have the potential to devastate a brand's image, even when the allegations later prove to be false.

Tommy Hilfiger fought back. Immediately on learning of the NCA allegations, it began its own internal investigation then published detailed responses on its corporate website. As stated on the site, "We believe in fair labor practices, and strive to assure that workers employed by the independently owned manufacturers who make Tommy Hilfiger products are treated with dignity and respect. This commitment means maintaining programs which seek to ensure appropriate working conditions and procedures in factories that produce Tommy Hilfiger clothing. . . . The cornerstone of our programs is our Code of Conduct. Formalized in 1997 and printed in 35 languages, the Code of Conduct incorporates internationally recognized labor standards, and outlines Tommy Hilfiger's expectations concerning the conditions under which its products should be made. Compliance with our Code of Conduct is assessed through a worldwide monitoring program. Since 1997, this program has included inspections in hundreds of factories in over 45 countries conducted by auditors working for third-party audit firms. We will continue to strive to have our Code of Conduct respected, and to have our products made under fair labor conditions."[12]

When Tears of Contrition Are Not Enough

The sweatshop travails of perky morning-show hostess and clothing manufacturer Kathie Lee Gifford are now legendary in the literature of labor law abuse. Thanks to Gifford's celebrity status, the issue of labor abuse instantly became a subject of national debate.

In 1996, a series of investigations by members of the National Labor Committee, a not-for-profit watchdog group whose stated mission is to protect worker rights throughout the world, exposed labor law abuses in substandard facilities in Honduras and Manhattan that produced Gifford's "Kathie Lee" line of blouses. After an initial attempt to defend herself, Gifford countered the accusations with an unusual public relations move: too distraught to visit the grimy Manhattan sweatshop, the teary-eyed Gifford sent her husband, Frank (and a barrage of media camera crews), to the factory to hand out $300 checks to the abused workers.[13]

But she was in the news again just a year later when authorities arrested the owner of three Manhattan factories contracted to produce Kathie Lee clothing and charged him with labor law violations. State Attorney General Dennis Vacco said conditions at these locations "resembled something out of a Charles Dickens novel," with laborers sometimes working 24 hours straight and not being paid for weeks at a time.[14]

In an attempt to control a firestorm of negative publicity, Gifford hired a first-rate public relations firm to transform her image from sweatshop owner to labor activist and antisweatshop crusader. She aligned herself with leaders in Congress, New York Governor George Pataki, and President Clinton to advance laws that addressed labor abuse. Gifford also established an independent monitoring program to check working conditions at her factories and weeded out over 100 factories in 16 countries that did not meet fair standards.[15] The public relations efforts worked; within months, Gifford was lauded as a leading advocate of workers' rights.

That is, until 1999 when, yet again, Gifford found herself the focus of labor abuse allegations. This time two employees from a factory producing Kathie Lee branded apparel in El Salvador testified that factory conditions there were harsh and unfair. More over-the-top public relations efforts followed (at one press conference, a teary-eyed Frank Gifford accused the head of the National Labor Committee, Charles Kernaghan, of making his children cry).[16] Clearly, the Kathie Lee brand had been tainted by the media reports of repeated abuses.

Taking Responsibility for Labor Abuses: Nike Bounces Back

In October of 2001, Nike CEO Philip Knight presented a corporate responsibility report to shareholders in response to the public uproar over reports that the company employed children as young as 10 in its factories in Pakistan and Cambodia.

"We blew it," the report stated, continuing, "By far, our worst experience and biggest mistake was in Pakistan." Although Nike purported to have strict age guidelines in place, Knight admitted that these standards were often difficult to verify. The chairman was blunt: "One mistake can brand a company like Nike as a purveyor of child labor."[17]

Unfortunately for Nike, Knight was right about his predictions. The company's critics remained vigilant in their determination to pressure Nike to change its ways of doing business with its Asian partners. A grassroots international boycott of Nike products began to grow. At colleges and universities doing business with the sports giant, administrators were pressured by students to hold the company to higher standards. Nike was ridiculed in such popular culture outlets as the comic strip "Doonesbury" and filmmaker Michael Moore's documentary *The Big One*.[18] No matter how many millions the company poured into its trendy advertising campaigns that featured popular sports icons, the spectacle of abused workers and child labor was devastating the company's image. It was time for Nike to publicly announce its good will and determination to adhere to global standards of fair trade and responsible conduct.[19]

Nike transformed its labor practices and pledged to open its Asian factories to public inspection from labor and human rights groups. In addition, the company raised to 18 the minimum working age in its footwear factories, increased its efforts to ensure air quality at those facilities, and seriously addressed other issues raised. The company also created a senior management post to oversee corporate and social responsibility issues.[20]

When Abuse Is Widespread—The Not so Sweet Story about Chocolate

While certainly pervasive in the textile and apparel industries, exploiting labor in the name of global trade can occur anywhere and in any industry. And sometimes it takes a concerted effort by the entire industry to change abhorrent practices.

A 2000 BBC investigative report revealed that a good deal of the chocolate we savor was being produced by child slaves on Ivory Coast cocoa farms. This devastating report claimed that hundreds of thousands of African children—some younger than 12—were being sold into slavery on these farms, where they were starved, beaten, and forced to work 100-hour weeks with no pay.[21]

As public awareness of this purported atrocity grew, so did pressure on the world's leading chocolate manufacturers. With the Ivory Coast supplying 43 percent of the cocoa beans produced worldwide each year, most major chocolate companies were customers. By June 2001, the U.S. House of Representatives responded to public outrage by voting to consider a "slavery-free" labeling system for chocolate products.[22]

The industry responded with teeth bared and fists out. Fearing the effects such legislation would have on their bottom line, the Chocolate Manufacturers Association, representing Hershey's and M&M Mars, which control two-thirds of the U.S. market, as well as other companies like Nestle and ADM, mounted a massive lobbying effort to fight off the bill. Using two former Senate majority leaders—Republican Bob Dole and Democrat George Mitchell—to lobby their former colleagues, chocolate manufacturers succeeded in blocking the bill.[23]

Even so, they couldn't ignore public scrutiny. Being in cahoots with child slavery was definitely not good for maintaining a positive brand. The industry took immediate steps to counteract public backlash.

Creating a Public-Private Partnership

First, they signed the Harkin-Engel Protocol, a program agreed to by U.S. and foreign manufacturers that aimed to eradicate the worst forms of child labor in the West African cocoa supply chain within four years.[24] Second, the industry established the International Cocoa Initiative, which shares the same mandate and includes representatives of industry, international labor, consumer, child rights, and antislavery organizations. Third, industry leaders pointed out that they had already been engaged for a number of years in efforts to support sustainable cocoa growing in West Africa in partnership with the U.S. Agency for International Development, CABI Bioscience, the International Cocoa Organization, the International Institute for Tropical Agriculture (IITA), and farmer groups.[25] Finally, the chocolate industry hired the IITA and the International Labor Organization to conduct their own investigation. That probe resulted in a 2002 report finding that "the vast majority of farmers in the region grow cocoa responsibly; no instances of slavery or forced labor were found on the more than 4,500 farms surveyed."[26]

By heeding the cries of the consumer, the chocolate industry took the reins and reversed prior practices, enhancing both the lives of cocoa workers around the world and its image as a protector of human rights in West Africa.

Politics and Gourmet Java: Starbucks and the Fair Trade Issue

The fair trade movement has gathered steam in recent years, largely due to a push by consumers concerned with how their products are produced abroad.

In the early 1990s, the Starbucks Coffee Company expanded its moderate Seattle operations into a national phenomenon. Almost overnight, Starbucks shops were popping up in every urban cranny, bookstore, airport, and shopping mall. As the company began hawking coffee beans from "exotic" third-world countries as luxury items, frappe-frenzied consumers happily stood in lines to spend upward of four bucks for a cup. But it wasn't just the coffee they were buying—it was the coffee *experience* that Starbucks had so masterfully branded as something cool and hip. This experience, aimed at the under-40 consumer, featured jazzy background music, exotic-sounding beverage names, and wireless Internet that invited hanging out. Starbucks had succeeded in turning the act of drinking coffee into an indulgent experience that spoke directly to the emotional perception of young consumers who saw the purchase of "designer" goods as a reward they richly deserved.

Ironically, it was this very branding that would ultimately threaten to boomerang back in the face of the Starbucks company.

Coffee prices on the global market were kept relatively stable until 1989, when an international agreement that restricted import and export volumes in an effort to promote stability in coffee bean growing countries fell apart. By 1992, an oversupply of production had helped drive prices down significantly. Meanwhile, as coffee became associated as a luxury item in the West, a grassroots awareness began to spread about the plight of third-world agriculture workers in the coffee industry—most of them living substandard lives of poverty and debt.[27]

The public eye was soon fastened on American coffee importers—with Starbucks, as the world's largest specialty coffee roaster, in the forefront. Fair trade activists, including students, religious groups, and labor unions, began to pressure the java giant to sell "fair trade" coffee. Fair trade products typically come from small-scale producers whom buyers pay a minimum price sufficient to cover production costs but also a premium designed to help local growers and manufacturers invest in health, educational, environmental, and other projects. In return, the producers commit to not using child or forced labor and using environmentally sound growing methods.[28]

With a purchase price of 50 cents per pound for coffee and retail prices of upward of $3 per cup, Starbucks had been pocketing huge profits annually. As public awareness grew, however, Starbucks executives found themselves facing a potential public relations catastrophe. How could they continue hawking their product as progressive and hip while activist campaigns shoved the faces and stories of impoverished coffee farmers in the face of American consumers?

Although it could have meant serious decreases in profit, Starbucks agreed to partner with the fair trade program. In 2000, the company introduced Fair Trade Certified coffee in all of its stores, more than 2,300 at that time.[29] By 2005, Starbucks was purchasing 11.5 million pounds of fair trade coffee a year and partnering with fair trade social programs around the world.[30]

Far from losing money, Starbucks managed to spin the situation into a positive story about the company's good will. In a brilliant public relations move, Starbucks showcased itself as a purveyor of fair trade and a friend to oppressed third-world farmers. Corporate talking points soon included language that spoke about the importance of building mutually beneficial relationships with coffee farmers and coffee communities. The result was happy Starbucks customers who would pay premium prices for coffee that helped poor farmers.

STEWARDS OF THE EARTH—TRADE AND THE ENVIRONMENT

If labor rights advocates were in the vanguard of the corporate social responsibility movement, those seeking to protect the environment were not far behind, and today the two issues are inextricably linked within the larger concept of corporate social responsibility. In the modern global village, you're just as likely to land on the front page for violating environmental regulations as you are for labor rights—maybe even more so considering how widespread and devastating the effects of an incident can be on public health.

Perhaps the best example of this is the Bhopal disaster of 1984, which bears the unfortunate distinction of being the worst industrial catastrophe of all time. While the event managed to raise public consciousness about government and corporate responsibility, it was also the catalyst that alerted industry to the crucial necessity of setting up systems to ensure strong environmental controls.

This terrible wake-up call occurred at Union Carbide India, Limited, a pesticide plant in Bhopal, India, when 40 tons of toxic gas was released into the atmosphere after a holding tank overheated. Thousands of deaths and injuries were caused by reaction to the toxic gas—as well as during the panicked melee that followed as tens of thousands of citizens attempted to flee the area. The deaths of thousands of others have been reported in the years that followed, purportedly as a result of exposure to the deadly toxin.[31]

The Union Carbide Corporation and its then-chairman Warren Anderson sprang to action, offering millions of dollars in aid to the relief fund, sending an international team of medical experts to assist in research and treatment, and offering to build a hospital in Bhopal.[32] The company also launched an aggressive campaign to investigate the cause of the accident, ultimately concluding that the gas leak was the result of deliberate sabotage.[33]

But the blame quickly shifted to Union Carbide itself as outside investigations uncovered evidence that pointed to Union Carbide's liability in the incident. Ultimately, the company paid $470 million in damages to the government of India and its chairman Warren Anderson was declared a fugitive from justice by Indian courts after he failed to appear in a criminal case against him and Union Carbide.[34] The company was eventually sold to Dow Chemical, which continues to endure protests for it to clean up the contaminated site.

SOCIAL RESPONSIBILITY IN SOURCING

Events like the ones highlighted previously illustrate a crucial point: There is no separation in the court of public opinion between your product, your brand, and your company's behavior and its leaders. In today's globalized society, public opinion is fueled by information collected and disseminated by the investigative media, non-government organizations (NGOs), bloggers, and watchdog groups. In order to thrive in the information age, global companies must put systems in place to avoid human rights and environmental violations throughout the supply chain, not only because it is the moral thing to do, but also because it is the only way to survive in an increasingly transparent world. And, in the event that an issue does come up, there must be a predetermined system in place to address the public's concerns swiftly and in an honest and forthright manner.

It is this business reality that should govern your approach to good corporate citizenship. Shout it from the rooftops, print it in your literature, and upload it onto your website: Your company must clearly and firmly state its commitment to labor rights and safe environmental practices. The statement should come from the highest ranking executive in your organization and be drilled into the head of every employee—from the CEO to the chief of sourcing to the rank and file members of your global team. Each employee should receive a copy of your firm's labor and environmental policy and it should be posted in all work areas—both domestically and abroad.

Pretty words will only get you so far, though—you've also got to put your money where your mouth is. In a world of multinational supply chains that means not only upholding your standards among your own employees but also enforcing them with respect to those you do business with. It's all well and good to make a strong commitment to doing right by workers and the environment, but the public has to see that that commitment extends further than your own front door.

One of the strongest controls you can establish with respect to ensuring that your entire supply chain adheres to your company's standards is to memorialize your position with regard to labor and environmental rights in your contractual arrangements with partners, vendors, contractors, and subcontractors. By prequalifying contractors and vendors, you can weed out any parties that have engaged in unscrupulous practices in the past. Contracts should clearly state what practices are unacceptable and severe economic sanctions should be agreed to in the event there are any violations, with a right to pull all production from a factory or to cancel a purchase contract should violations be found. If there is any hesitation to sign a social responsibility agreement on the part of potential offshore partners, take that as a sign that this is likely a company you should pass on. Demand that your contractors undergo a precertification process and agree to periodic inspections.

Any factories you source from must agree to rigorous inspections from qualified preshipment inspection organizations. Inspections to ensure workplace compliance as well as the existence of environmental controls should occur before work is commenced and then periodically through a system of spot inspections throughout the contract term. There are a number of organizations—both commercial and not-for-profit—that provide worldwide inspection services. Be sure that the company you choose has a stellar reputation in the international community, is familiar with the local labor and environmental laws of the country where the factory is located, and is familiar with the requirements of relevant trade agreements. In addition, the preshipment inspectors should have a thorough understanding of your organization's internal policies.

In some instances, industry leaders have banded together to form their own self-monitoring associations dedicated to promoting social responsibility in sourcing. In the aftermath of the sweatshop scandals of the 1990s involving Kathie Lee and other apparel brands, companies cooperated to form Worldwide Responsible Apparel Production (WRAP), which promotes strict labor standards for its textile and apparel industry members and demands that participants follow rigorous inspection protocols. WRAP's goal is to independently monitor and certify that factories comply with standards for lawful, humane, and ethical working conditions through a rigorous monitoring protocol and by requiring its members to comply with detailed practices and procedures. Members agree to comply with workplace laws and regulations in all locations where they conduct business, are prohibited from using involuntary or forced labor or child labor, provide a workplace free of harassment or abuse, adhere to fair compensation and benefit standards, and comply with laws regarding hours of work. In addition, workplace discrimination is prohibited, freedom of association is promoted, and health and safety standards must be upheld. Members agree to comply with environmental rules, regulations and standards, as well as the rules governing customs and international trade and security. (See www.wrapapparel.org.)

This pattern has been followed for environmental issues as well. Recognizing the urgent need to present a unified response to the Bhopal incident, members of the chemical industry founded the Responsible Care program in 1985. Under this global initiative companies, through their national associations, work together to review and improve health, safety, and environmental performance—and to communicate with stakeholders about their products and processes.[35] In the United States, companies participating in this program (which is required for membership in the American Chemistry Council) have lowered their emissions of toxic chemicals by over 75 percent and have enjoyed an employee safety record nearly five times higher than the average for the domestic manufacturing sector.[36]

Seek out industry organizations that fit your products or services. And in the event violations do occur, take immediate steps to remedy any infractions. Self-policing is the only way your company can ensure that its offshore counterparts are adhering to your conduct requirements. The vast majority of missteps occur not through the malicious activities of the brand owner, but from the unscrupulous or negligent practices of contractors and subcontractors in the supply chain.

FREE TRADE AGREEMENTS AND CORPORATE SOCIAL RESPONSIBILITY— FORGING A LINK

While industry-developed policies and programs are useful, you also need to make sure you're in compliance with government-established standards. These have become increasingly prevalent in recent years and have become key elements in many bilateral and multilateral trade agreements.

This was not always the case. Politicizing the link between trade agreements and corporate social responsibility had always been anathema to trade professionals, both in private industry and governments around the world. The prevailing thought was that labor policy and trade policy were separate. Often, developing countries fought U.S. intervention in social and labor issues, seeing them as a U.S. labor movement ploy to discriminate against their products. For developing nations, the ability to compete by offering cheap labor gave them their seat at the globalization table. Forcing them to adopt the labor protections afforded to workers in a structured industrial society was seen as foreign imperialist interference of the worst kind. Many developing nations adopted the attitude that they could take care of their own without big brother's intervention, thank you very much.

But as globalization increased the ranks of multinational corporations setting up shop in countries where labor standards weren't traditionally as high as they were in the West, and as the information age made it easier to keep track of and publicize working conditions in these Third World factories, the momentum began to swing in favor of labor rights advocates. Things came to a head in 1999, when the culture clash between what emerging nations see as interference and the labor movement considers legitimate human rights issues was front and center during the infamous WTO ministerial meeting in Seattle. Tens of thousands of protesters took over the streets and effectively shut down the talks. The images and words of the demonstrators took the world by storm and got people thinking: Why were domestic jobs being outsourced to developing nations that exploited workers to keep labor costs down? How could the industrialized country workforce compete with this type of unfair competitive edge? And who was protecting the workers in these far-off facilities who had no choice but to accept substandard pay in unsafe working conditions?

One of the most important issues brought to the forefront of public discourse by the events in Seattle was whether there was going to be a formal linkage between trade and corporate social responsibility. The majority of trade professionals were adamantly opposed to such a link. But President Clinton made a historic speech in Seattle, for the first time acknowledging that the nexus between labor, the environment, and trade already existed. In that speech, the president said, "I believe the WTO must make sure that open trade does indeed lift living standards—respects core labor standards that are essential not only to worker rights, but to human rights. . . . To deny the importance of these issues in a global economy is to deny the dignity of work—the belief that honest labor fairly compensated gives meaning and structure to our lives." He went on to acknowledge that many developing nations were wary of a link between labor rights and trade: "I am well aware that a lot of the nations that we most hope to support—the developing nations of the world—have reservations when the United States says we support bringing labor concerns into our trade debate. And I freely acknowledge that, if we had a certain kind of rule, then protectionists in wealthy countries could use things like wage differentials to keep poorer countries down—to say, okay, you opened your markets to us, now we'll sell to you. But you're selling to us and we want to keep you down, so we'll say you're not paying your people enough. The answer to that is not to avoid this labor issue—not when there is still child labor all over the world; not when there are still oppressive labor practices all over the world; not when there is still evidence in countries that ordinary people are not benefiting from this. The answer is not to just throw away the issue. The answer is to write the rules in such a way that people in our position, the wealthier countries . . . can't use this as an instrument of protectionism."

The president then proceeded to acknowledge that environmental issues had taken a position at the forefront of the globalization debate. "We must work to protect and improve the environment as we expand trade. . . . Again, I know there are some people who believe my concern and the concern of the United States about the environment is another way that somehow we can keep the developing countries down. That is not true. There are basically two great clusters of environmental issues facing the world today. First, there are the local issues faced primarily by the developing nations: healthy water systems and sewer systems, systems to restrict soil erosion and to otherwise promote the public health. It is in everyone's interest to help those things to be installed as quickly and efficiently as possible. But the real issue that affects us all, that prompts my insistence that we put this issue on the agenda, is global warming and the related issue of the loss of species in the world as a consequence of global warming. . . . There is now clear and compelling scientific, technological evidence that it is no longer necessary for a poor country growing rich to do so by emitting more greenhouse gas emissions. Or, in plainer language, a nation can develop a middle class and develop wealth without burning more oil and coal in traditional manners."[37]

Clinton knew what many in the trade were just beginning to admit—the court of public opinion had already spoken. All you had to do was scan the streets of Seattle to know that the days of drawing a line in the sand between labor and environmental practices and free trade had come to an end. By popular demand, and expressed in the protest chants of those marching on Seattle, global trade had become irretrievably linked to human rights, social responsibility, and the environmental protection movement. The time had come to formally acknowledge that these elements of international trade were inseparable.

It was during these turbulent times that our firm was negotiating Cambodia's first textile and apparel quota agreement with the United States, the first to formally connect trade and labor rights. Since that landmark accord, every free trade agreement that the United States has entered into has contained some elements addressing labor issues in the context of trade benefits.

The 1994 North American Free Trade Agreement does not itself contain labor rights provisions, but the three member countries signed on to the North American Agreement on Labor Cooperation (NAALC) as a side pact to the FTA. The first international agreement on labor to be linked to a U.S. free trade agreement, the NAALC requires the trading partners to enforce domestic labor standards and laws without interfering in each other's national labor systems. Along with protecting and enforcing workers' rights, the NAALC creates dispute resolution mechanisms related to labor conflicts.

NAFTA was also the first "green" multilateral trade agreement. But that distinction didn't come easily for the parties involved. In 1991, three environmental groups, led by the advocacy group Public Citizen, filed a complaint against the Office of the U.S. Trade Representative, essentially setting in motion a chain of legal and administrative maneuvering that would culminate in a side agreement, the North American Agreement on Environmental Cooperation (NAAEC). The thrust of the agreement is to ensure that the parties—Mexico, Canada, and the United States—protect the environment, agree to pursue sustainable development based on cooperation and mutually supportive environmental and economic policies, and work cooperatively to conserve, protect, and enhance the environment, including wild flora and fauna.

Each of the FTAs the United States has since become a party to has some mechanism for establishing labor standards and addressing environmental concerns, although the nature and extent of these mechanisms can vary depending on whether the Democrats or Republicans control Congress and/or the presidency. As these agreements continue in force, governments are cracking down on violators. Recently, the Jordanian government targeted companies it found to be engaging in labor law violations, reportedly a result of increased scrutiny of human rights issues in Jordan under the auspices of the labor provisions contained in the U.S.-Jordan FTA. Under that agreement, the United States can impose sanctions for failure to meet the trade pact's labor standards. The allegations of abuse were brought to light by the New York-based National Labor Committee.[38] Wisely, the government and industry members in Jordan have addressed and continue to address these concerns, reflecting the importance of such production in Jordan.

As workers' advocates, the environmental lobby, industry, and governments continue to debate international standards, the global trader is faced with increasingly complex issues as world trade breaks down barriers and obscures borders. From a practical standpoint, international business is ultimately tasked with finding a balance between open trade and fair labor and environmental practices. Trade agreements, public policy, and government enforcement may all contribute to the complexity of the issues, but in the final analysis, global business must answer to the customer and the standards imposed by the court of public opinion are turning out to be the strictest of all.

Tenets of Global Trade

1. *You and your brand are inseparable.* Your company's greatest asset is its brand. Your products and services cannot be separated from either your tangible brand—logos, domain names, trademarks, patented technology, copyrighted works—or your firm's less tangible, but equally important, reputation.

2. *You must be vigilant in protecting your intellectual property both at home and abroad.* Intellectual property protection begins with an examination of your IP portfolio. Next, take steps to record your IP in every country in which you are doing business or may branch out to in the future. Additionally, it is a good idea to protect your brand in regions known to be centers of counterfeiting and pirating.

3. *You must be vigilant in enforcing your IP rights.* Be mindful of your choices for business partners and work with an IP professional to confirm each party's understanding of who owns rights to what. Use government programs such as CBP's recordation program and ITC's 337 investigations to guard against infringement. And finally, resort to litigation to protect your rights if necessary. It is ultimately your responsibility to protect your brand's integrity.

4. *Protect your worldwide reputation by strict adherence to labor and human rights standards.* No industry is immune

from exploitative labor practices. Be vigilant in your dealings with offshore partners and contractors. Adopt strict standards for your organization and demand that any company you do business with adheres to your standards on your terms. Employ professionals to shore up contractual arrangements, employ professional inspection services, and, if applicable, join industry associations that promote fair labor practices.

5. *Take steps to ensure your global partners adopt environmental safeguards.* Make sure every company you contract with follows your company's code of conduct with respect to environmental controls. Pay attention to local laws and take a long-term view of your industry's activities and do all you can to reduce your company's environmental impact.

6. *Pay attention to labor and environmental safeguards built in to trade agreements.* The failure to meet specified standards can result in not only a loss of reputation, but also a loss of trade benefits. It never pays to take shortcuts.

7. *Remember that the court of public opinion is stronger than any government tribunal.* Often, governments set up minimum standards that have more to do with compromise among negotiators than adhering to socially responsible sourcing criteria. Fueled by the investigative media, NGOs, watchdog groups, and bloggers, news of missteps can be blasted around the world in no time. Your personal and corporate reputation is your greatest asset. Protect it at all costs.

MAINTAIN HIGH ETHICAL STANDARDS

Sometimes the lines between ethical and unethical business practices and even legal and illegal activities can become blurred in a global business context. What is considered an expected gratuity in one country may be counted as an illegal bribe in another. Transparency rules require that commercial documents be accurate and verifiable, but often the global entrepreneur must rely on information provided by companies within the supply chain that might not conform to local and international laws and ethical standards. Your company must establish its own standards of acceptable conduct and enforce those standards through internal monitoring systems. Even the appearance of impropriety must be avoided to protect your company and its officers and shareholders from negative publicity, government sanctions, and the possibility of criminal prosecution. Ethics, social responsibility, and other issues of corporate governance are vital components to forging successful and long-lasting international business relationships.

BRIBERY IN BENIN

In 1998, the country of Benin hired San Diego-based defense contractor Titan Corporation to build and operate a wireless telephone network in the impoverished West African nation.[1] To convince the former French colony to consent to a project management fee hike, the company hired an agent to help with the negotiations. According to the Securities and Exchange Commission (SEC), this agent was really a business advisor to Benin President Mathieu Kerekou. The SEC charged that in 2001, Titan funneled more than $2 million through this agent to the president's reelection campaign, including reimbursing him for T-shirts showing the president's picture and voting instructions.[2] Two $500,000 payments were invoiced as "consulting services" and were wired to the agent's off-shore account in Monaco. Other payments were made in cash.[3] The government also claimed that Titan made a gift of a pair of $1,850 earrings to President Kerekou's wife.[4] In addition, Titan was accused of falsifying documents in connection with business dealings in Nepal, Bangladesh, and Sri Lanka, as well as failing to maintain an effective system to discourage the bribing of public officials.[5]

Finally, after several years of investigation, the company pleaded guilty in 2005 to three felony charges related to foreign bribery and tax law violations and agreed to pay a total of $28.5 million in fines and penalties, the largest amount ever imposed on a public company for violating federal laws prohibiting bribery of foreign officials.[6]

THE CASE FOR ETHICS IN BUSINESS

The global marketplace can look and feel a lot like the Wild West. Operating in a world lacking a shared platform of business codes of conduct and laws and judicial procedures that define standards of ethical conduct, companies can find themselves in a grey zone where ethical standards vary from region to region—or worse—from country to country. Basic business principles such as accountability, transparency, and uniform standards of compliance can appear negotiable. In addition, the standards of ethical conduct that apply to the company's home country do not always apply abroad. If bribery, slave wages, environmental savagery, and worker abuse are accepted in the host company, how should the foreign company respond? Certainly, the opportunity to profit monetarily from a lack of ethical standards has tempted many a transnational company to violate its own ethics and mores. On top of all of this, practices that comply with Western codes of ethics might be a hard sell in the host country.[7]

Where some multinational companies may view the lack of operational and ethical standards as an opportunity for monetary gain and knowingly partake in the corruption, others have been proactive about creating systems and strategies to avoid unethical dealings. The advent of recent ethics scandals and a push by governments to beef up enforcement activities has spurred many of the leading transnational companies to take a proactive stance to create worldwide standards for corporate conduct.

The accounting scandals of the past decade and the public outcry that accompanied them spurred the U.S. Congress to pass new corporate accountability laws. The September 11, 2001, terrorist attacks added to this increased scrutiny, prompting the government to take steps to require that companies keep a sharper eye on what is going on in their back offices, on their factory floors, and throughout their supply chains. Federal agencies from the FBI to the SEC have ramped up their enforcement efforts in recent years, resulting in record numbers of prosecutions,

fines, and jail time for violators. This, in turn, has galva-
nized the trade community toward self-regulation. This is
particularly the case for the larger multinationals whose
sourcing and logistics tentacles reach across the globe.

Through organizations like the International Chamber
of Commerce (ICC), the international business community is banding together to create its own self-monitoring
systems to stave off an increase in government control of
internal business dealings. Self-regulation and corporate
accountability are the catchwords of the day. Government
consortiums like the Organization for Economic Cooperation and Development (OECD) are also attempting to
standardize ethical standards among member nations. To
survive and thrive in today's global marketplace, entrepreneurs must keep ethics at the forefront of every business
decision. It's just good business, after all.

Smart companies understand that there is a line
drawn in the sand when it comes to fair business
practice—and crossing that line can carry huge risks.
Charges of child labor, environmental insensitivity,
bribery, and worker abuse will most likely be revealed by
the countless human rights groups set up to expose
abuse in the global marketplace. The result? Huge public
relations disasters for the company that allegedly committed the perceived abuse. Many large companies have
endured these public embarrassments.[8]

The shortsightedness of engaging in unethical or illegal practices to realize immediate profits can send a company's value spiraling downward in the long run. Today,
equity management firms count ethics and social responsibility as primary indicators of the future success of a company. Corporate governance is considered a key factor in
assessing a company's value and future growth and viabil-

ity. Some of the world's most trusted investment advisors are giving thumbs down to companies with a poor ethical track record, even if other economic indicators point to what should be a sound financial future.

For example, in a study published in 2006, investment firm AllianceBernstein concluded that the behavioral aspects of a company's governing culture are just as important as traditional financial indicators such as transparency and adherence to international accounting standards. Companies making initial public offerings (IPOs) need to assure investors that they have established a reasonable level of socially responsible governance as well. An ethical image and an active self-monitoring program are key indicators of how a company will fare, especially in the context of emerging markets. Investors are cautioned to look beyond raw numbers when assessing a company's potential for investment and take issues of corporate governance into account. What constitutes sound governance principles has changed. Having a code of ethics, adhering to an equal opportunity policy, and setting forth socially responsible policies such as prohibitions on underage labor are reaching equal status with financial indicators in assessing a company's overall rating. Good numbers can be deceiving, and without these intangible governance factors, AllianceBernstein is loath to recommend a company for investment. According to the report, "From an investment perspective it is important to know when a stock is undervalued as opposed to when it is cheap for a reason. Bad corporate governance is a good reason for stocks to look cheap."[9]

Corporate governance issues have also risen to prominence for investment organizations like the International Finance Corporation (IFC), the private sector arm of the

World Bank. The IFC finances investments in private sector businesses in relatively high-risk developing countries. When deciding whether to make a particular investment, the IFC uses a methodology developed in-house to evaluate the quality of the target company's existing corporate governance measures. It also works with that company through the course of its involvement to further improve those measures on the basis of industry best practices.[10]

FORGING ETHICAL STRATEGIC PARTNERSHIPS

Creating an ethical paradigm for your company's operations begins with establishing an ethical framework that not only all your employees adhere to, but that your strategic partners embrace as well.

In global business, strategic partnerships are ruled not only by law but also by common goals and interests. It is up to you to set the tone. If your global strategic partners understand your company's culture of compliance, morality, and ethical behavior, they will be on notice that this is the only context in which they can do business with you. If you don't set that standard from the very beginning, if you don't impose 100 percent accountability on all your business associates, it's bound to catch up with you eventually.

Setting the ethics bar to a higher level engenders goodwill among your own officers, managers and staff, your contractors and subcontractors, and the customers who buy your products or services. Once lost, positive brand image is hard to regain. So even though there is a likelihood that someday in some unexpected context an ethical or legal violation will occur, establishing your business as an ethical enterprise will go a long way to retain your reputation, even if missteps occur.

Setting the Ethics Bar

Experience shows that at some point in your global business dealings, someone affiliated with your organization will likely succumb to errors in judgment and may even violate U.S. or foreign laws. It may occur as a result of an activity performed by someone within your organization or it will occur somewhere up or down the chain of supply. If egregious and far-reaching, it may expose your company to adverse media attention, shareholder consternation, or even civil and criminal penalties. Certain types of ethical malfeasance can even land the principals of a company in jail.

Maybe an overzealous middle manager will look the other way when false invoices are presented to customs to lower duty payments. Or someone in your organization will funnel excess funds to a government official in a developing country to help secure a lucrative contract after some cabinet secretary making $4,000 a year lets it be known that your competition is willing to grease its way to the deal. It seems like everyone else is doing it, so why shouldn't you?

When you get in over your head in a global context, it can be extremely difficult, if not impossible, to control the damage. That is why it is so important to establish a written code of conduct that reveals your company's culture of unimpeachable ethics, to establish a system of corporate governance infused with ethical precepts that are communicated up and down the chain of supply.

Could an error or omission still occur regardless of your best efforts? It is highly likely that it will. And that is precisely why you must set the highest ethical standards for yourself, your strategic partners, your officers, your employees, and your agents. Just think of the damage that could result if you fail to set the bar as high as you can. Titan had no firm policies regarding corporate ethics. It was run with the eye on the prize rather than any ethical restraints on what constituted an acceptable process to get to the prize. An established code of conduct might have swayed the offending actors from carrying out their bribery scheme. At the very least, their actions would have been seen as a violation of an established corporate policy, which could have been used as a mitigating factor to be taken into account during penalty assessment.

Establish a Code of Ethics

The Titan case was unusual, to be sure. Most companies do not spend millions of dollars greasing a foreign government's wheels to gain lucrative contracts or to alter fee arrangements. But sometimes less flagrant acts can still run afoul of federal law and accepted ethical standards. With international business transactions, it is not always that easy to know where principled practices stop and unethical behaviors begin.

In some countries, for instance, providing a gratuity to the customs officials processing your paperwork is status quo. You are expected to tip these people the same way you would tip a baggage handler or a taxi cab driver. In other countries, social conventions mandate that you offer a gift to a dignitary and/or his spouse. Consultants and agents are regularly used abroad to forge relationships and help seal deals. It is important to effectively monitor the actions of your contractors to ensure that they don't expose your company to charges of misdirection of funds, bribery, or other unethical conduct.

In establishing a code of ethics, company officials must conform to the ethical standards required by law, follow the dictates of their own conscience, and be cognizant of public perceptions that can affect the attitudes of the consumer in the marketplace. The place to start is with an understanding of the ethical standards to which companies are held by both the law and the international business community.

The Foreign Corrupt Practices Act

The Foreign Corrupt Practices Act of 1977 (FCPA; 15 USC §§78dd-1, et seq.) has reemerged as a powerful weapon in the U.S. government's ethics enforcement arsenal. Much in the way Sarbanes-Oxley was a response to the Enron accounting scandal and other fiascos of the late-1990s, the FCPA was enacted following a slew of bribery scandals involving hundreds of U.S. companies in the mid-1970s. Generally speaking, the FCPA bars U.S. companies from bribing foreign officials in order to secure or maintain a business relationship, whether directly or through an agent or other intermediary. The law was expanded in 1998 to prohibit foreign companies or individuals from facilitating such bribes while in the United States. The FCPA also requires publicly traded companies to keep books that accurately portray corporate transactions and to develop and implement effective internal accounting controls.

Penalties for violating the FCPA can be severe. In addition to paying hefty criminal and civil fines, offenders may be barred from doing business with the federal government, blocked from obtaining export licenses, suspended from the securities exchange, and ruled ineligible for programs administered by the Overseas Private Investment Corporation and the Commodities Futures Trading Commission.

They can also be sued under the Racketeer Influenced and Corrupt Organizations Act (RICO), which allows for triple damages, as well as various other federal and state laws. In some instances, individuals responsible for the violations are sent to jail.

Titan was prosecuted and fined under the FCPA, among other statutes. And while that fine was certainly hefty, no sanctions were imposed against individuals in the company. Not so in other cases. In October 2004, a federal court convicted two former senior officials of American Rice Inc. for bribing Haitian officials as part of a scheme to obtain lower duty rates on rice exports to that country.[11] A company vice president was convicted of submitting shipping documents that underreported the volume of the company's rice shipments to Haitian customs officials. Those officials had been paid in cash by local ARI employees to look the other way. The company then recorded the bribes, at least 12 payments totaling $500,000, as routine business expenditures. The company saved $1.5 million in Haitian customs duties.[12] The vice president was sentenced to 37 months in prison. The company's president was found to have had knowledge of the operation and received a 63-month prison sentence.[13]

It is apparent that the government is moving full steam ahead in its antibribery enforcement activities. The U.S. Department of Justice conducted more foreign bribery investigations between 2001 and 2006 than it did in the preceding 20 years. In March of 2006 alone, the department launched 11 new FCPA probes.[14]

Setting Up FCPA Compliance

What steps can you take to make sure you don't run afoul of the FCPA?

First, create and implement an FCPA compliance plan that establishes clear ground rules, provides for regular monitoring, and allows you to respond to problems before they get out of hand. Titan's fate was sealed once it was determined that the company had no standardized policies or procedures covering prohibitions on bribery or foreign agent oversight.

It is imperative that you reduce your company's ethics policies to writing and disseminate them in your standard operating procedures manuals. Designate a corporate officer to oversee monitoring and reporting efforts, including making sure that all financial transactions are properly recorded. Establish guidelines for hiring and retaining foreign agents and include your antibribery policy and other ethics rules in all contracts.

Because the FCPA has a number of grey areas, such as allowing some "facilitation payments" as long as they do not directly influence the outcome of a service or decision by a foreign government employee, erring on the side of caution is always the best tactic. If in doubt, don't do it, or at a minimum consult with counsel before proceeding along any lines that could be suspicious. And if your compliance officers do discover activities that could potentially be in violation of the FCPA, take immediate remedial steps to correct the problems. Above all, keep impeccable accounting records for all payments to foreign government entities or officials, charities, agents, consultants, and other third parties.

MULTINATIONALS AND A PUSH FOR SELF-REGULATION

Multinational corporations, through business organizations and trade associations, are pushing for heightened

self-regulation of ethical behavior. Nongovernmental organizations and the United Nations are also working to
write uniform rules to discourage corruption in international business dealings.

In 2005, the ICC's Anti-Corruption Commission published its revised Rules of Conduct to Combat Extortion
and Bribery. First drafted in 1977 in response to the same
corruption scandals that prompted Congress to pass
FCPA, the rules of conduct prohibit facilitation payments
and require that companies set up specific mechanisms
that allow their employees to anonymously report violations. The rules also prohibit bribes made on behalf of
ICC member businesses through agents or other interme-
diaries, foreign subsidiaries, joint venture partners, or outsourcing arrangements.[15]

The ICC has designed the rules of conduct to serve a
dual purpose. They are primarily aimed at encouraging
corporate self-regulation by showing proactive businesses
how to develop policies and procedures to prevent bribery
and ensure compliance with associated national laws. But
they have also served as a guide for individual nations and
multilateral organizations in their efforts to foster a culture of intolerance toward corruption through laws and
treaties. While the rules themselves are voluntary and not
enforceable, they embody a set of practices that have been
incorporated in a variety of forms, from company standards to international agreements.[16]

Transparency International, an organization formed in
1993 that is most known for its annual reports ranking
over 150 countries on how corrupt they are perceived to
be, first offered its Business Principles for Countering
Bribery in 2002. Like the ICC's rules of conduct, these
principles were created as a template to help companies

come up with their own antibribery programs. Transparency International also offers a more in-depth guidance document that provides additional information on the background and implementation of the principles, as well as a how-to guide that outlines a six-step process for companies that need more intensive help in creating antibribery policies and procedures and putting them into effect.[17]

The United Nations has also encouraged businesses to fight corruption, but in a more general way. Participants in the U.N. Global Compact, which was initially launched in 2000 to link businesses, civil society groups, and the United Nations in an effort to encourage corporate social responsibility around the world, agreed in 2004 (in the so-called 10th principle) that businesses have an obligation to work against bribery, extortion, and other forms of corruption and should develop specific policies and programs to this end. But the Global Compact provides few details on what these policies and programs should look like, instead emphasizing the sharing of information and best practices and collaboration through sectoral initiatives. It points participants to groups like the ICC and Transparency International for specifics on developing corporate compliance programs, although it has published in conjunction with Transparency International and the International Business Leaders Forum a guide outlining internal, external, and collective actions companies can take to implement the 10th principle.[18]

Bribery and other forms of corruption are just one part of the Guidelines for Multinational Enterprises issued by the OECD, which comprise principles and standards on topics such as labor and the environment, human rights, consumer protection, and competition.

The guidelines encourage companies to refrain from direct or indirect bribery; to develop training, management, accounting, and other systems designed to prevent bribery; and to encourage openness and transparency with the public to demonstrate their commitment to ethical behavior. Although the 39 countries that have signed on to the guidelines to date are obligated to promote their use within their borders, the guidelines are not legally enforceable and businesses may choose whether or not to follow them.[19]

The guidelines are designed to complement the two major international agreements against bribery and corruption—the OECD's Convention on Combating Bribery of Foreign Public Officials in International Business Transactions and the U.N. Convention Against Corruption—and the national laws that have been promulgated to implement them.

The OECD convention entered into force in February 1999 and has been ratified by all 30 member countries as well as six other nations. It requires signatories to criminalize in their national legislation the bribery of foreign public officials to obtain or retain business or other improper advantage in the conduct of international business (e.g., seeking preferential treatment with respect to government procurement contracts, regulatory permits, customs requirements, legislative initiatives, or court actions).[20] These laws must cover attempted as well as actual bribery, whether directly or through an intermediary, along with assisting others in offering or paying bribes. In addition, appropriate measures must be taken to prohibit accounting and recordkeeping activities designed to facilitate or disguise the bribery of foreign public officials. Liability is established for corporations as well as individuals. Countries are also obligated to provide prompt and effective legal assistance to other signatories pursuing a criminal investigation into violations of the convention, which are considered extraditable offenses.[21]

The U.N. Convention Against Corruption was adopted in October 2003 and took effect in December 2005. The U.N. Convention Against Corruption is broader in scope than the OECD pact and is the first international treaty addressing this issue. It covers the issues of prevention, criminalization, international cooperation, and asset recovery with respect to many different types of public as well as private (business to business) corruption. Signatories are required to criminalize corruption in its various forms; if doing so in certain areas is barred by existing domestic laws, they must consider amending those statutes to make the subject acts a criminal offense. The convention sets forth model policies that governments can follow to prevent corruption and encourage transparency and accountability. Countries are obligated to provide mutual legal assistance to other participants and to extradite offenders, similar to the OECD convention. They are also required to take concrete steps to facilitate the seizure of money, goods, or other proceeds from corruption and to return these assets to the nations harmed by it.[22]

IMPORTING AND EXPORTING: SELF-GOVERNANCE AND ACCOUNTABILITY

In addition to general corporate governance laws and regulations, companies involved in international trade need to make sure they are in compliance with statutory and regulatory requirements that specifically pertain to imports, exports, and related transactions. Many of these measures have changed over the past 10 to 15 years in a way that has increased the responsibilities and liabilities of traders.

Self-Monitoring Import Transactions

With the passage of the Customs Modernization Act (Mod Act), part of the law that implemented the North American Free Trade Agreement, which took effect December 8, 1993, the U.S. importing community was put on notice that it must be able to substantiate the legality of its import activities or face hefty fines and penalties.

The Mod Act shifted to the trade community much of the legal responsibility for ensuring compliance with applicable rules. To do this, it emphasizes that international traders exhibit reasonable care in complying with the rules and regulations governing international transactions and that they operate under a system of informed compliance. U.S. Customs and Border Protection is obligated to ensure that traders are provided with clear information about their legal rights and responsibilities, while importers, brokers, agents, and others are required to make their best efforts to comply.

One of the trade community's responsibilities under the Mod Act is to maintain and make available on request the necessary records to enable U.S. Customs and Border Protection (CBP) to properly assess duties, collect accurate statistics, and determine compliance with applicable legal requirements. Records include paper documents or electronic information normally kept in the ordinary course of business regarding imports, entries, in-bond merchandise, drawback, fees, and taxes—anything covered by the so-called (a)(1)(A) list (19 USC §1509(a)(1)(A)).

U.S. Customs and Border Protection is entitled to examine any of these records, which usually must be produced within 30 days of their request. Penalties for non-compliance are substantial: administrative fines of up to $100,000 for willful violations and $10,000 for negligent violations can be imposed for each release of merchandise, and entries can be reliquidated at higher duty rates. In addition, companies that fail to produce records or otherwise participate in an audit, investigation, or other proceeding may ultimately have their importations and deliveries suspended.[23]

There are always those looking to circumvent import rules for financial gain through various schemes. One example is dual invoicing, where the invoice presented to customs officials for duty calculation purposes reports a value for the merchandise that is lower than the one on the invoice submitted to the buyer for payment. But customs officials the world over have robust enforcement efforts in place to counter this practice, not only because it can defraud governments of revenue but also because it has been a popular way to launder money for international crime and terrorist organizations.

Penalties for dual invoicing therefore tend to be significant. A New York City company was assessed a criminal fine of $110,000 and its president was sentenced to two years in prison for a dual invoicing scheme designed to help smuggle restricted sturgeon caviar into the United States.[24] But as is often the case when a company breaks a law, the fallout from its involvement in criminal activity is often much more crippling than the financial setback of a fine. In one instance, a major apparel company with over $800 million in annual sales ultimately collapsed after it was convicted on dual invoicing charges, leading its major client to terminate the business relationship and making it impossible for the company to secure additional financing.

MINDING YOUR EXPORT TRANSACTIONS

Following a relative lull after the end of the Cold War, the U.S. government has ramped up its export enforcement efforts, increasing the amount of money, personnel, and resources dedicated to pursuing violations and handing out ever-larger penalties.

Exporters, freight forwarders, and others involved in sending goods, services, and technology outside of U.S. borders must comply with numerous requirements under the Export Administration Regulations, International Traffic in Arms Regulations, Foreign Assets Control Regulations, and other bodies of laws and regulations administered by various U.S. government agencies. Licenses for exporting and reexporting such items may be needed based on the nature of the product or service. For example, the import, export, reexport, and sharing of commodities, services, and technical data that are specially designed for military end-use may require a license. However, most items exported from the United States that require a license are so-called dual-use goods, which have military as well as commercial applications; but even everyday seemingly innocuous products may require a license if they are being shipped to a specially designated individual or entity, to a country of concern, or for a purpose that could harm U.S. interests. The transfer of controlled technology also poses significant compliance issues for U.S. companies and, depending on the circumstances, a license may be required before such technology can be legally transferred. In addition, licenses are also required for what are termed "deemed exports," that is, when controlled information or technology is released to a foreign national in the United States. Under this "deemed export" rule, if a license is normally required for the export of that information or technology to the intended recipient's home country, a license will also be needed to release or expose such information to the recipient in the United States.

As noted, exports may also be prohibited or restricted based on where the shipment is headed or the way it will ultimately be used. Export control agencies, primarily the departments of Commerce, Treasury, and State, maintain a number of separate lists of countries, organizations, and individuals of concern. These include people that have been denied export privileges, companies deemed to present particular risks due to past records of suspicious behavior or activities, international terrorists, drug traffickers and arms dealers, and countries named as state sponsors of terrorism. Exporters are expected to screen their transactions against these published lists, and are obligated to investigate and resolve any "red flags" associated with the parties to or the circumstances regarding their transaction before proceeding with the shipment. Proceeding with a transaction with knowledge that an export violation is about to occur is a serious violation in and of itself.

Similar to importers, exporters must accurately complete required paperwork and maintain sufficient records to demonstrate their compliance. The primary document associated with exports is the shipper's export declaration (SED), which is used to tally export statistics and help federal authorities enforce export laws. Other forms include export clearance records, applications for licenses, licenses issued by the various U.S. government agencies, requests for item classification, and inquiries as to which government agency exercises jurisdiction over the proposed transaction. Complete and accurate information must be provided on all such paperwork.

While it is generally the exporter who bears primary responsibility and liability for complying with applicable export rules and regulations, others have obligations as well. Freight forwarders and other agents hired to facilitate exports by obtaining licenses, preparing SEDs, and performing other tasks must do so as accurately as possible using the information they are given by the exporter and keep records to prove it. They are legally liable for the truthfulness of the forms they sign, even if they are relying on information provided by the exporter. Forwarders also are required to look out for red flags and make good faith efforts to address them before going ahead with a shipment.

Government efforts to enforce all of these requirements, as illustrated by the Department of Commerce's Bureau of Industry and Security (BIS), have taken a noticeable upturn in recent years. In fiscal year 2006, for example, the BIS Office of Export Enforcement issued $3 million in criminal fines and more than $13 million in administrative penalties along with 33 orders denying export privileges to various companies.[25] Export laws allow BIS and other government agencies to impose stiff penalties for civil and criminal violations—which can range from $50,000 to $1 million per violation, and include up to 20 years' imprisonment. The following examples highlight the emphasis enforcement authorities are placing on these crimes and how costly they can be.

One of the most common and therefore most frequently penalized violations is the failure to obtain an ex-

port license when one is required. A former North Car-
olina state senator was assessed an $850,000 criminal fine
and his Raleigh-based corporation Sirchie Fingerprint
Labs Inc. paid a $400,000 civil penalty for exporting var-
ious crime control equipment to China without the required license. Silicon Graphics Inc. paid a $1 million
criminal fine and a $182,000 civil penalty for the unli-
censed shipment of restricted high-performance computers to a Russian nuclear facility and the re-export of
computers from Switzerland to the United Arab
Emirates. Even after notifying BIS of its violations and
cooperating in the subsequent investigation, Lattice
Semiconductor Corporation had to pay a $560,000 civil
penalty for exports to Chinese nationals in the United
States, exports of technical data to China, and shipments
to that country of high-tech equipment without getting a
license.[26]

Another area of emphasis for government authorities
has been shipments to restricted entities or for prohibited
end-uses. Ebara International Corporation was given a
$6.3 million criminal fine and a $121,000 administrative
penalty for a scheme to export pumps controlled for antiterrorism reasons to Iran through an intermediary in
France. A man was fined $100,000 and sentenced to nearly
15 years in prison, and his forwarder spent six months in
jail, following a criminal investigation involving exports of
night vision equipment through Greece to the Hezbollah
terrorist group. An IBM subsidiary paid an $8.5 million
criminal fine and a $171,000 administrative penalty for
sending computers to a Russian nuclear facility despite
having enough information to know that they were likely
to be used to work on nuclear explosive devices. And DSV
Samson Transport, a New Jersey freight forwarder, was

assessed a $250,000 criminal fine and a $399,000 civil penalty for facilitating shipments to India that were controlled for nuclear nonproliferation reasons.[27]

Submitting false information in connection with an export can also be costly. International High Tech Marketing was fined $250,000 and assessed a $115,000 administrative penalty for using fraudulent invoices and SEDs.[28] BIS levied a $250,000 criminal fine and a $77,000 civil penalty on a California company, and a $12,000 criminal fine and an $88,000 civil penalty on its owner, for attempting to export to China a restricted thermal material used to insulate satellites without the required license and declaring on the SED that no license was required.[29] Pending Census Bureau regulations are expected to sharply increase the criminal and civil penalties that can be assessed for failing to file export information or filing false or misleading SEDs.

One method of supplying false information in particular, dual invoicing, has seen a sharp rise in enforcement. As is the case with imports, avoiding tariffs, taxes, and other fees by undervaluing exports is increasing and is receiving greater scrutiny around the world. A California company was fined $140,000 and required to forfeit $1.1 million in assets after pleading guilty to a dual invoicing scheme regarding exports of computer components to England and Ireland.[30] In August 2006, U.S. authorities helped dismantle an export undervaluation scheme that is believed to have denied Brazil over $200 million in import duties over the past five years. The exporters involved face penalties that could total millions of dollars, as well as substantial jail time for corporate officers, if they are convicted on charges of mail or wire fraud, money laundering, making false statements, and violating the FCPA.[31]

Importing and exporting issues can arise in the context of almost any international transaction and every country and territory has its own rules and regulations for international transactions. The problems outlined here are just the tip of the iceberg when it comes to delineating the myriad issues that can occur when moving cargo into and out of countries throughout the world. The global trader is well advised to become an expert in the rules and regulations affecting his or her company's transactions and set up a global import/export compliance program that reflects the basic concepts of reasonable care and informed compliance.

TRADE PROGRAMS AND COMPLIANCE

Importers and exporters taking advantage of free trade agreements and preferences are at risk of running afoul of the complex eligibility rules and accompanying documentation requirements to substantiate eligibility for the import duty breaks these programs provide. Even acts of simple negligence can cause big problems. The rule of thumb is that without substantiation of eligibility the preference will be disallowed. And in some cases, the failure to present evidence of eligibility can result in draconian fines and penalties. A large multinational corporation was hauled into court by U.S. Customs after refusing to pay tens of millions of dollars in fines for allegedly filing false claims of NAFTA eligibility and not maintaining sufficient documentation to support those claims.[32] Other companies have been retroactively denied the benefits of a program and assessed back duties with interest. In some cases, the failure to adhere to free trade agreement (FTA) requirements has resulted in the seizure and forfeiture of merchandise due to allegations of illegal transshipment.

ESTABLISHING A CORPORATE CODE OF CONDUCT AND COMPLIANCE

Understanding the ethical, legal, and regulatory challenges of operating a transnational business is just the first step in establishing a corporate code of conduct and compliance. Your company's policies regarding the ethical and compliance behavior that is expected from employees and outside business associates must be documented in a clear and unambiguous fashion and publicly available to any interested parties. While there are no set rules for exactly how your code is constructed, it is useful to look at the practices of companies that have led the way in establishing ethical business practice rules.

One such company is Levi Strauss & Company, which produces and sells clothing around the globe. Levi's leaders implicitly understand that upholding ethical business standards on a global basis is the only way to conduct good business. Levi's message—maintaining respect for human dignity and worker rights is just plain good citizenship no matter where you are doing business—is readily evident by its code.

The company's Global Sourcing and Operating Guidelines state that Levi Strauss will "seek to identify and utilize business partners who aspire as individuals and in the conduct of all their businesses to a set of ethical standards not incompatible with our own." These guidelines help the company to "select business partners who follow workplace standards and business practices that are consistent with LS & CO.'s values and policies." They are also "applied to every contractor who manufactures or finishes products" for Levi Strauss.[33]

This code of conduct is made known to every host country with which Levi Strauss forges a relationship. The company leaves nothing open to interpretation, stating: "We will not initiate or renew contractual relationships in countries where the legal environment creates unreasonable risk to our trademarks or to other important commercial interests or seriously impedes our ability to implement these guidelines."[34]

Motorola publishes a comprehensive Code of Business Conduct on its website. The beginning statement of its chairman and CEO sets the tone of the document: "The Code of Business reaffirms what each Motorola employee stands for: Doing the right thing. Every day. No excuses."

Now that's a pretty clear and powerful statement. The document goes on to enumerate the company's policies on just about every conceivable business practice regarding responsibility and accountability to shareholders, customers and consumers, and governments. It is clear about its commitment to compliance with anticorruption laws like the FCPA and provides specific rules about how to handle solicitations for gifts, bribes, and facilitation payments. The six-page document leaves little ambiguity regarding what is and what is not sanctioned in Motorola corporate culture.[35]

As more and more companies invest serious resources in developing codes of corporate conduct, the scope of the behavior covered by those codes has expanded as well. One example is protecting the environment, an important ethical concern for today's consumers, who are more aware than ever before about the effects of industrial practices on natural resources as well as their own quality of life. Hong Kong-headquartered Esquel Group, under the direction of Chairman and CEO Marjorie Yang, has taken on a leadership role when it comes to promoting corporate environmental responsibility. In facilities scattered throughout China, Malaysia, Vietnam, Mauritius and Sri Lanka, the company employs close to 50,000 workers who produce over 60 million shirts a year for branded apparel companies such as Hugo Boss, Abercrombie & Fitch, and Land's End, as well as major retailers including Nordstrom. Despite this enormous industrial footprint, Esquel's stated social responsibility policy emphasizes the need to continuously find ways to foster environmental consciousness and awareness at all levels of the organization. Recently, the company announced the opening of a new environmentally friendly weaving mill in China, which is outfitted with state-of-the-art energy-saving equipment and a new wastewater treatment facility capable of processing and recycling 24,000 tons of wastewater a day. Clearly, Esquel is an industry leader when it comes to promoting strong environmental protection policies.

One Step Further—Ethics Executives

Of course a company's statement of values is only as meaningful as the steps it commits to taking to enforce those values. Many of the companies implicated in the corporate governance scandals of the past decade had established ethical standards policies that all employees were expected to adhere to. But when ethics is everyone's job, sometimes it ends up being no one's job. A lack of effective oversight and enforcement can be just as bad as having no policies or standards at all.

As a result, a growing number of companies are creating new executive positions that are specifically responsible for ethics, compliance, and corporate governance issues. Some are seeking to avoid a recurrence of the troubles they've run into with shareholders and government agencies in the recent past. But many are taking this route in order to prevent such problems, spurred on by laws and regulations enacted over the past 15 years that prescribe tougher corporate punishments for white collar crime but also allow penalties to be eased if companies can show they had a good ethics program in place. About half of the largest companies in the United States and Canada are reported to have installed ethics executives. The Ethics and Compliance Officer Association says its membership has shot up 25 percent since 2003 and now totals more than 1,000, including more than half the companies in the Fortune 100 as well as nonprofit organizations, municipalities, and industry organizations.[36]

Hanesbrands Inc. is a good example of how businesses are responding to this trend. Stressing that one of its most important assets is the reputation of its brands, products, operations, and employees, the company created the new position of vice president of corporate social responsibility to oversee all of its efforts in the areas of ethics, compliance, environmental protection, and philanthropy. Hanesbrands promoted from within to fill the new post, naming a former associate general counsel and vice president of risk management. Some experts say such a strategy can offer substantial benefits to a company consolidating corporate responsibility functions into a single office for the first time because it can help ensure that the new executive has a knowledge of your values and operations, sufficient issue experience to hit the ground running, and the trust and confidence of the rank and file.

At a time when the public, the media, and the government are all watching corporate behavior more closely than ever before, chief ethics officers are quickly becoming like iPods: 10 years ago nobody knew what they were, but now people can't imagine how they ever got along without them. The advantage of having a corporate ethics officer in this kind of environment is clear. It's not enough anymore to just be a good guy; now you also have to make sure everyone knows you're a good guy, from consumers to business partners to government regulators. Putting a single executive in charge of ethics can go a long way toward achieving these objectives—he or she can spearhead efforts to instill a culture of high standards throughout your company, serve as a safe point of contact for employees seeking to head off potential violations, and speak with authority to stockholders, the media, and others when issues do arise.

Ethics, values, and social responsibility are the cornerstones of any company's compliance policy. But organizations involved in international business need to also get down to brass tacks when formulating compliance procedures. Much in the vein of current standards imposed by laws such as Sarbanes-Oxley, all global trading companies, whether publicly traded or not, should create international business compliance manuals that cover their day-to-day operations in manufacturing, sourcing, importing, exporting, and transporting goods across international borders. Rules for international business are complex, often program and item specific, and the onus is placed on the global trader to understand the applicable laws and regulations and comply with them.

Tenets of Global Trade

1. *Strong ethics translate into good business.* Accountability, transparency, and high standards of ethics and compliance are an absolute business necessity in today's global marketplace. Not only are watchdog groups and the government on constant lookout for un-

scrupulous business practices, but shareholders and investors are beginning to take corporate governance issues into account when valuing a business. Ethical and compliance missteps can land principals in jail, result in hefty fines and penalties, damage your reputation and your brand, and devalue your enterprise.

2. *Forge ethical strategic partnerships.* Establish an ethical framework and demand compliance from your employees, agents, vendors, suppliers, and partners. Setting a high ethics bar engenders goodwill from your business associates and goes a long way to helping you retain your good image, even should missteps occur.

3. *Understand corporate accountability laws.* U.S. federal laws such as the Foreign Corrupt Practices Act are designed to discourage bribery of foreign officials and promote honest international business transactions. Gain an understanding of the laws governing acceptable international business practices and make sure that your officers, employees, and overseas agents adhere to the strict letter of the law. If an activity seems wrong, it probably is. Consult with experts before potentially crossing an ethics line.

4. *Become involved with the international business self-regulation movement.* Organizations like the International Chamber of Commerce, spurred on by multinationals, are fostering a worldwide culture of intolerance toward corruption. Play your part in encouraging social responsibility across the world. It makes sound business sense and is becoming a global trade necessity.

5. *Develop compliance protocols for import and export operations.* The Customs Modernization Act and Export

Administration Regulations place the onus on importers and exporters to self-monitor their international trade operations. Become intimately familiar with the complex laws, regulations, and rules that govern your transactions and create global compliance procedures for all your international trade transactions.

6. *Memorialize your company's code of ethics and compliance practices in writing.* Develop a strong statement of ethics for your company that details what practices are and are not acceptable. Make sure that all your employees, contractors, and strategic partners are aware of your policies and take measures to enforce your code.

7. *Appoint a leader.* Designate an executive to be specifically responsible for ethics and other corporate responsibility issues, whether by rearranging existing duties or creating a new position altogether. Consolidating these functions under a single office can boost efforts to establish and maintain high standards throughout your corporate structure and help promote your company's public image.

STAY SECURE IN AN INSECURE WORLD

Security has always been a primary concern for those engaged in global business. Companies operating internationally must take into consideration the safety of employees and partners while traveling and living abroad. The issue of safeguarding cargo from damage, theft, and loss, as well as from becoming an instrument of drug trafficking, is also a serious one affecting all forms of international commerce. In recent years, though, the word "security" has taken on a new dimension for the international business community. The September 11, 2001, terrorist attacks were the catalyst for sweeping changes in the way international trade operates around the world. No longer a matter restricted to individual business interests, security now requires new levels of transparency throughout the entire international supply chain. New security dynamics are not only necessary to protect international borders from terrorists, but have become an integral part of conducting business around the world.

SECURITY IN A POST-9/11 WORLD

On Tuesday, September 11, 2001, many of us were just arriving at work when American Airlines Flight 11, hijacked by al Qaeda terrorists, crashed into the North Tower of New York's World Trade Center at 8:46 A.M. Just a few minutes later, United Airlines Flight 175 crashed into the South Tower. Soon the news spread that the Pentagon in Northern Virginia had been hit and that another plane was downed in Pennsylvania.

Half a decade later, the effects of the attacks on the nation's psyche are still being felt. And while the tragic loss of human life is certainly not to be diminished in any way, it is important to acknowledge that the events of September 11 also were an assault on global commerce.

Immediately following the attacks, all U.S. ports of entry, land, sea, and air, were put on Level One Security Alert. For a brief period, all U.S. ports were shut down. All trade into and out of the United States came to a standstill.

By September 12, the ports had been reopened, but the effects of this level of security were becoming abundantly clear to the trade community. The increase in the frequency and magnitude of inspections and scrutiny at ports of entry was causing agonizing backups and already devastating some U.S. and foreign businesses. At Canadian crossing points, wait times for trucks carrying goods into the United States, which had averaged 10 to 20 minutes before September 11, were increased to more than 10 hours. By September 14, auto plants in Michigan were beginning to shut down production for lack of parts.

The government needed to get commerce up and flowing again. According to then-Customs Commissioner Robert Bonner, who had only just arrived in Washington on September 10, one of the government's first orders of business was to find ways to secure the borders and ports of entry without stifling the flow of trade and shutting down the U.S. economy. In November 2001, at the Customs Trade Symposium in Washington, DC, Commissioner Bonner proposed that the trade community and the government work together in the fight against terrorism. The Customs-Trade Partnership Against Terrorism—C-TPAT—was born, a logical extension of already existing cargo security initiatives.

DO YOU KNOW WHERE YOUR CARGO IS?

The need to keep your cargo secure in an insecure world was nothing new. Prevention of theft and piracy had long been a priority for global enterprise. Swashbuckling pirates once terrorized the high seas plundering hapless ships and their crews. Casting aside cutlasses for AK-47s and rocket-propelled grenades, today's pirate gangs terrorize the international shipping industry in high-speed boats, costing the United States alone a whopping $15 billion a year in loss of cargo. According to industry estimates, worldwide losses from shipping theft total approximately $50 billion annually.[1]

Of course, cargo theft can occur at every step in the supply chain and can affect nearly every product. More than $25 billion worth of goods are believed to be stolen annually in the United States.[2] The California Trucking Association estimates that losses from thefts of tractors, trailers, and cargo approach $1 million a day. Due to the costs associated with investigations and insurance payments, it is estimated that companies must spend 10 to 15 times the value of each loss to make up for it.[3]

The illegal drug trade is also a threat to cargo security. Drug trafficking is a lucrative industry; a U.N. report claims that it accounts for almost 10 percent of all international trade or more than $400 billion a year. The illegal drug market in the United States is one of the most profitable in the world and a large percentage of these drugs enter the country in freight containers. Millions of cargo containers enter the United States by rail, truck, and ship every year, a figure that is expected to continue to rise in the years ahead. Drug smugglers have plenty of opportunity to conceal voluminous quantities of cocaine, heroin, marijuana, and methamphetamine.

Sanctions for bringing concealed controlled substances into the United States can be severe. Penalties range from $1,000 per ounce of heroin, morphine, cocaine, and opium to $500 per ounce of marijuana.[4] The fines alone can permanently cripple some companies. In addition, the carrier used to transport illegal narcotics can be seized and forfeited under federal law. In an infamous example, U.S. Customs used its authority in 1984 to seize an Eastern Airlines jet in Miami, after discovering three pounds of cocaine hidden away in an area containing avionics equipment. Clearly, along with the potential for seizure and forfeiture and severe monetary penalties, the damage to a company's reputation can be substantial. Drug busts make headlines.

While the issues affecting cargo security prior to 9/11 had been aggressively addressed by the government and the private sector, the 2001 terrorist attacks have taken the issue of cargo security to a whole new level. The question became, how do you keep your business and merchandise secure in an environment where a weapon of mass destruction secreted in a container holding your merchandise, packed by your factory, and transported by your chosen carrier is ultimately your responsibility? As a global trader, you are now tasked with securing your cargo against loss, thwarting would-be drug traffickers, and ensuring that your business practices do not open the door for international terrorism. It sounds a little extreme, but the international trade community has taken on more and more of an enforcement role over the past 20 years and the increased responsibility being placed on the private sector to prevent terrorist attacks in the past few years shows that these high levels of responsibility are continuing.

The reality of security in today's global trade environment is that complete transparency in international trade is an absolute requirement. This transparency necessarily extends throughout the supply chain. The company responsible for bringing goods across borders must be able to ascertain who is supplying what to whom throughout the manufacturing, shipping, and distribution processes. Security must be ensured every step of the way. A failure to provide evidence that the entire supply chain is secure through complete transparency can not only result in goods held up in transit and increases in costly and time-consuming inspections, but can in effect cause trade to all but come to a standstill.

THE PRIVATE SECTOR FIGHTS BACK AGAINST THE ILLEGAL DRUG TRADE

Beginning in the 1980s, the government's war on drugs took a new turn. Recognizing that the most effective way to secure cargo and the borders against illegal drug trafficking was with the cooperation and buy-in of the trade community, U.S. Customs formed active partnerships with the private sector, offering both incentives and sanctions to encourage the trade's complicity. The Carrier Initiative

Program (CIP) and the Super CIP, the Business Anti-Smuggling Coalition (BASC), and the Americas Counter Smuggling Initiative (ACSI) were designed to give the trade a stake in the government's antitrafficking initiatives.

Established in 1984, the CIP encourages sea, land, and railroad carriers to improve their security practices to prevent drug smuggling. Under the voluntary program, carriers with route systems that are considered high risk for drug smuggling sign agreements with U.S. Customs and Border Protection (CBP). Customs and Border Protection provides on-site training and facilities inspections for the carriers, who, in turn, agree to do everything they can to ensure that their facilities and conveyances are secure. Carriers with extraordinarily high-risk route systems are eligible for the Super CIP program. One of the major benefits of these programs is that carriers who demonstrate high levels of compliance can qualify for reduced penalties if narcotics are discovered on one of their conveyances. To date, CBP has entered into more than 3,800 CIP agreements and 27 Super CIP agreements with carriers.[5]

Initiated in 1996 by the private sector, BASC is a voluntary program set up to examine and monitor the supply chain—from manufacture through the shipping process. Although there are no government-mandated requirements associated with BASC, commercial trade industry participants are expected to utilize security standards that will decrease the chance that their companies will be used to smuggle contraband into the United States. The BASC emphasis is on the complete supply chain and introduces transparency as a new anti-smuggling, and post 9/11, as an antiterrorism, requirement. More than 200 companies participate in BASC.[6]

According to CBP, ACSI offers "a more comprehensive approach" to dealing with the problem of smuggling through the commercial cargo supply chain. Under ACSI, the agency is working with the trade industry and governments throughout Latin America. Customs and Border Protection sends officers to partner countries to help exporters, manufacturers, carriers, and others to implement effective antismuggling programs. They also work with foreign law enforcement and other officials to improve government efforts against smugglers.[7]

These types of government-to-trade partnerships have resulted in a clear win-win for both sectors. Law enforcement receives much-needed assistance in its efforts to combat trafficking, and the trade receives assistance with formulating and applying anti-smuggling plans and a mitigation of penalties should best efforts fall short.

A CONTINUATION OF GOVERNMENT-TRADE COOPERATION

The success of these public-private partnerships helped form the basis for the evolution of C-TPAT. Like the programs discussed earlier, C-TPAT is a voluntary government-private sector partnership. But unlike the other programs, it is clear that C-TPAT is fast becoming voluntary in name only. The incentive for joining is faster clearance with limited inspections and disruptions. The other side of the coin—more inspections resulting in delays and disruption in the importation process for companies not participating—turns this voluntary program into a trade necessity.

The C-TPAT application and verification process can take as much as a year to complete and there is no doubt that it places additional financial burdens on importers and their suppliers. First, applicants sign a memorandum of understanding in which they agree to follow C-TPAT guidelines. Next, they create a document or manual detailing their existing security practices, including those of their suppliers. Customs and Border Protection reviews this document and either accepts the company's current processes or makes recommendations for improvement. The last step is an onsite inspection by CBP officials who verify that the processes and procedures furnished to Customs are actually being followed.

Just months after the program was introduced, seven major corporations—Target Stores, Sara Lee, Motorola, General Motors, Daimler-Chrysler, Ford, and BP America—had already signed on. By September 2006, more than 6,000 companies, including importers, customs brokers, terminal operators, carriers, and foreign manufacturers had become certified C-TPAT partners. It is apparent that joining this "volunteer" program is becoming the status quo. In fact, suppliers to the big retail chains understand that participation is fast becoming a requirement of being selected or retained as a vendor. Most of the big retailers now require that their suppliers either be C-TPAT members or meet stringent security standards.

Because it reaches deep into the entire supply chain, C-TPAT is designed to create transparency at every stage of the manufacturing, purchasing, and transportation/logistics process. By being able to trace goods from inception, through all international movements, to entry into the United States, both private companies and CBP can greatly reduce the likelihood that any particular container or shipment conceals instruments of international terrorism.

U.S. Customs and Border Protection has made no bones about its agenda with C-TPAT. By getting the multinationals to buy in to the concept, a large portion of the international supply chain will have to follow suit if they want to continue their relationships with the biggest companies. As the international supply chain sets up security measures, smaller companies who rely on the same factories and carriers will necessarily get on board. The alternative to C-TPAT participation can be a death knell for companies. Getting your goods where they need to be when they need to be there means life or death for commercial enterprise. Most, if not all, global trading companies will eventually choose life.

SECURITY AND CUSTOMS AROUND THE WORLD

If leading multinational companies and customs agencies around the world have their way, the concept of a business-to-government partnership to create global supply chain security will soon permeate practically every customs territory throughout the world. The World Customs Organization (WCO), consisting of 170 member nations, is responsible for harmonization of worldwide customs procedures. The WCO, with the assistance of many of these multinationals, has developed a Framework of Standards to secure and facilitate global trade. The Framework's aims are to establish uniform worldwide standards for supply chain security at a global level while promoting the continuous and seamless movement of goods through secure international trade supply chains.

Much in the same manner the WCO establishes uniformity in tariff treatment of goods around the world through creation of a harmonized tariff, the organization is now striving to harmonize security measures. One of the cornerstones of its strategy is to encourage a customs-to-business partnership through the cooperation of Authorized Economic Operators (AEOs).

Authorized Economic Operators will be similar to C-TPAT participants in that they will be required to document supply chain security measures and monitor the flow of trade from manufacture through distribution. The WCO, in conjunction with the trade community, will establish the validation processes to gain AEO status. Once the status is obtained, benefits such as expedited customs clearance and a reduction in inspections and import/export delays will be provided.

ADDITIONAL GOVERNMENT SECURITY PROGRAMS

In a push to secure the nation's borders from terrorism while still allowing for the smooth flow of trade, the U.S. government has created a number of additional security programs. Some have caused importers to reconfigure processes to comport with new requirements while others have significantly increased CBP's presence both at U.S. and foreign ports. The Container Security Initiative (CSI), the 24-Hour Rule, and new detection technologies are just a few of the programs CBP has instituted since 9/11.

Under CSI, CBP works with customs officials at foreign seaports to identify and examine high-risk maritime containerized cargo destined for the United States. By the end of September 2006, 50 foreign ports covering more than 82 percent of maritime cargo shipped to the United States were participating in CSI.

The Advance Manifest Rule, or 24-hour rule, requires that details about an incoming shipment be furnished to Customs 24 hours before the sea container is loaded onto the outbound vessel. This requirement has caused some consternation among importers, who now must procure entry documentation, and ensure that it is accurate, sometimes weeks before the shipment is due to arrive. This program is being extended to all modes of transportation.

The government is also employing large-scale X-ray and gamma ray machines and other radiation detection devices in cargo screening. The president's FY 2007 budget earmarks $157 million to secure next-generation detection equipment.

The increase in supply chain transparency and accuracy and timeliness of documentation has bolstered the government's efforts to find alternatives to securing borders through 100 percent inspections, an impossible task given the volume of merchandise entering the United States every day. These measures have also bolstered the trade community's incentives to employ commonsense measures to keep cargo secure. The added "carrot" of faster clearance, coupled with the age-old problems of preventing theft and drug trafficking, mean that more and more companies are seeing ancillary benefits of increased security measures.

BOTTOM LINE BENEFITS OF CARGO SECURITY

According to a 2006 Stanford University study, investments in supply chain security are reaping benefits above and beyond the original purpose of securing cargo and avoiding becoming an instrument of terrorism. In many instances, beefing up security is resulting in cost reductions in other areas, higher revenues, and growth leading to positive ROI. In fact, business justifications for investing in supply chain security are showing that the benefits can outweigh the initial cost/investment.[8]

There can be no doubt that the events of 9/11 have affected the cost of doing business for global traders. Airfreight costs as well as commercial insurance premiums have increased significantly since 9/11. The subsequent roll-out of new government-driven security initiatives that require importers to meet strict disclosure requirements and take responsibility for security throughout the supply chain have placed an additional financial burden on many companies. But in many cases, the study concludes, the collateral benefits of new security measures are proving to result in ample benefit to a company's bottom line to justify their inclusion in standard operating procedures from a business perspective.

New security measures are improving efficiencies, with tangible cost-saving results becoming more and more apparent. For example, the Stanford researchers found that a tightening of controls often results in a reduction in the frequency of product handling. Less handling means fewer errors, improved process compliance, and reductions in process deviations. With fewer steps in the supply chain process, cycle times from order to shipping are lessened, fewer personnel are needed to oversee cargo movement, and there are fewer shipping delays.

Many companies are also seeing improvements in inventory management processes, according to the study. By incorporating tighter controls on the ordering and receiving process, businesses are seeing reductions in quantity discrepancies as well as reductions in inventory levels.

The study also points out that greater inventory management has produced a marked reduction in tampering for some businesses, resulting in decreased amounts of theft and loss. Tightening procedures to ensure proper inventory tracking and control of receiving and shipping is key to preventing loss of cargo. Enforcement of operator accountability has become an industry standard and more cargo companies are hiring security officers to enforce such policies. These officers are responsible for checking security seals, keeping unauthorized people out of the area, tracking employees as they enter and leave cargo areas, and opening all trailers designated as empty before they leave the lot. By employing devices such as Global Positioning Systems (GPS) and Radio Frequency Identification (RFID) to keep track of containers, and bolstering other security measures such as container locks and high-security seals and using driver teams, businesses are not only keeping the supply chain safe from terrorism, but foiling would-be hijackers and thieves. Some companies are even reporting that a result of employing better security practices is a reduction in the magnitude of counterfeiting.

A vigilant employee and contractor background screening program is not only a critical feature of a successful antiterrorism program, but serves to reduce instances of theft and loss. And the documentation transparency and timeliness required under regulations such as the 24-hour advance manifest rule, have caused improvements in visibility throughout the supply chain. Companies are now reporting, the study says, that the improvements in the timeliness and accuracy of shipping information are translating into cost savings because data inaccuracies or deficiencies are addressed immediately as a condition of entry.

The Stanford study also finds that companies are experiencing an increase in resilience, the ability to define and solve problems. And any businessperson will tell you, the faster a problem is addressed, the less cost to remedy the problem. The collateral consequences of improved security are also showing up in the customer relations arena. Many businesses report an increase in customer confidence and satisfaction now that there are tighter controls on the supply chain.

Since heightened supply chain and cargo security is a necessary part of international business, the companies that will thrive in this new environment are the ones that use the new requirements to their own strategic advantage.

DO YOU KNOW WHERE YOUR DATA IS?

Hardly a news program goes by without another report concerning a major corporation or government agency falling victim to data theft. In the past few years, Bank of America, Wachovia Corp., AT&T, MasterCard, Chase, Time Warner Inc., Citigroup, and even the Veterans Affairs Department have all experienced major breaches of data security. Indeed, data security concerns have become so pervasive that the Federal Bureau of Investigation reports that businesses spend about $67.2 billion a year combating viruses, spyware, theft, and other computer-related crimes.[9] According to a 2005 Federal Trade Commission report, identity theft affects nearly 10 million people each year and has staggering costs—$5 billion for consumers and nearly 10 times that for businesses.[10] The stories are legendary—and astounding in their scale.

In 2005, for instance, a hacker stole information on more than 40 million Visa, MasterCard, American Express, and Discover credit card holders from a transaction processing company in Tucson.[11] In 2006, the federal Department of Veterans Affairs reported a computer containing personal records on more than 26.5 million veterans had been stolen from an employee's home.[12] In 2005, hackers broke into AT&T's systems affecting the credit card info of 19,000 customers,[13] and Bank of America reported a loss of records on 1.2 million credit cards handed out to federal employees that same year.[14]

Data vulnerability is a fact of doing business that all companies—large and small—have to learn how to manage and be responsible for. According to most reports, though, they're not doing a very good job. A 2006 survey by the Ponemon Institute, a company specializing in privacy and information management research, and Vontu Inc., which focuses on helping companies avoid data loss, found that during the preceding year 81 percent of responding companies had reported losing at least one laptop computer containing sensitive information. Sixty-four percent said they had never inventoried the consumer and employee data in their possession.[15]

One of the common denominators in data fraud is the phenomenon of outsourcing data processing to foreign companies, especially in India, the Philippines, and China. U.S. companies outsource an estimated $3 billion a year in business processing, including banking information, tax files, insurance claims, medical files, and credit card data. While businesses certainly benefit from cheap labor, they are also more removed from the operational procedures in these foreign outposts. U.S. privacy laws cannot be enforced in foreign locations and it becomes more difficult to trace the attacks to their source in countries where sanctions are more lenient.[16]

While companies devote large amounts of funds toward preventing external intrusions, some argue that the greater threat comes from their own employees. Over 70 percent of data theft is estimated to come from internal sources but only 1 percent of corporate security budgets are spent on guarding against such threats.[17] With software and networks becoming increasingly more secure, cyber-criminals are targeting inside personnel to help execute their attacks. Employee layoffs, high staff turnover, political unrest, and weak or nonexistent fraud regulations all present potential threats.

Of course employee stealing is not limited to offshore outsourcing. No matter where a company processes, stores, and transmits its data, it remains highly vulnerable to theft. Information security has become a top concern for most companies—and not just because of the financial ravages the company can suffer from the theft. According to one survey, nearly 60 percent of consumers polled said they had stopped or would be willing to stop doing business with companies that lose their personal information. The same survey showed that the total cost to a company for a data breach averages $14 million. In one instance of careless handling of customer records, an entire brand reputation can be destroyed.[18]

Intense media scrutiny and heightened public concern have inspired companies to take action, demanding more accountability from information technology managers and others higher up the ladder. AOL's chief technology officer resigned after it was disclosed that the company had publicly released data on searches done by about 650,000 of its online subscribers.[19]

What's the bottom line when it comes to data security?

Companies must recognize that the privacy and protection of their customers will become a competitive differentiator in the cybertheft struggle—and take aggressive measures to prevent it. This means spending real time and money on implementing comprehensive security solutions, restricting sensitive data, initiating vigilant employee background screening programs and regular review sessions, disciplining staff when breaches occur, and creating information management plans and policies. Eventually, it might also mean that companies will need to inform clients as to where their data is held and processed.

KEEPING SAFE ABROAD

As an international trade attorney and consultant, I log more miles traveling the globe each year than I care to count. My travels often take me to places where an obviously American businessman is in danger the minute he steps off the plane. Sometimes the danger is hard to decipher and even the most experienced travelers can make serious mistakes.

During a trip several years ago to Cambodia, I was late for an important client meeting just two blocks away from my Phnom Penh hotel. Briefcase in hand, I started down the stairs at the front of the hotel to make my way to my meeting. Just as I landed on the last step and was about to go onto the sidewalk, a security guard sent by the client I was to meet with grabbed my arm and motioned to an armored car waiting for me at the curb. Sometimes, in many developing countries, even a short, unprotected two-block walk can be a risk.

As global trade expands, so do instances of kidnapping and extortion. In many of the world's leading danger zones, the kidnapping of foreign corporate executives and employees is a growth industry. Any company exploring foreign business ventures should be aware of this very real threat and take aggressive measures to prevent it—and be prepared to skillfully manage the situation if it happens.

Although the Middle East has quickly become a hot spot for such abductions, Latin America—with Colombia in the lead—has remained responsible for more than 80 percent of all ransom kidnappings. In Colombia alone, more than 3,500 kidnappings are reported each year, with over $250 million in ransom payments made annually.[20] In these countries, the business of kidnapping has become a way of life for thugs, rebel armies, and even the police force. But this menace is certainly not limited to Latin America. African nations have also become kidnapping hot spots with the explosion of Western interest in the African oil industry. During one month in 2006, for instance, 17 people working for oil companies that operate in the Niger Delta, most of them foreigners, were seized for ransom.[21]

So what's a company to do?

Forward-thinking companies are initiating comprehensive crisis management planning programs. These strategies include consideration of specialized insurance that helps pay for ransoms, negotiators, security, and other related expenses.[22] One insurance and benefits firm reports that U.S. citizens with so-called K&R (kidnapping and ransom) coverage, which is relatively inexpensive (e.g., $500 a year for a $1 million policy for a small company, or $50,000 for $25 million worth of coverage for a multinational corporation),[23] are four times more likely to survive a kidnapping than those who don't.[24] Despite this, only 60 percent of the 500 biggest corporations in the United States carry K&R policies.[25]

Many companies are now establishing response teams to deal specifically with terrorist acts such as kidnappings. These teams are often comprised of personnel from the human relations, legal, public relations, and finance departments, as well as communication specialists who relay information to kidnappers, the media, and other sources.[26]

A comprehensive crisis management planning program should address more than just kidnapping and extortion. Companies should be prepared to assist employees and their families in cases of terrorist attacks, emergency evacuation, natural hazards, and environmental disasters. These programs should include rigorous training designed to help employees assess the local cultural and political situation of the countries they will be traveling in. The majority of Fortune 500 companies have programs in place to help employees understand the culture of their overseas locations.[27]

Hiring security protection for executives traveling in danger zones has become de rigueur for many American companies. Major corporations now provide private security details for their top executives, and often send personnel in advance of a trip to recon high-risk areas and travel routes.[28]

Finally, all corporations doing business overseas should be aware of the Overseas Security Advisory Council (OSAC), a federal advisory committee that fosters the exchange of operational security information between American companies with overseas operations and the State Department. Since being established in 1985, OSAC has developed into a dynamic vehicle for effective security cooperation, with more than 3,500 U.S. companies, universities, and non-governmental organizations as active participants. OSAC's 34-member governing board in Washington is supplemented by over 100 country-level councils around the world. Corporations consult OSAC reports for information ranging from security issues to travel advisories to understanding regional customs and laws.[29]

Tenets of Global Trade

1. *Security requires transparency throughout the supply chain.* Securing cargo has always been a prime concern for international traders. Piracy, theft, and drug smuggling can wreak havoc on your company's revenue, resulting in lost sales or hefty penalties. Since the 2001 terrorist attacks, the stakes to keep your cargo secure have risen dramatically. Today, failing to secure your cargo can result not only in monetary loss, but loss of life as well. Complete transparency throughout the supply chain is an absolute requirement of doing global business in a post-9/11 world.

2. *Participate in trade-government partnerships.* Getting your goods where they need to be when they need to be there means life or death for commercial enterprise. Private sector partnership with government enforcement agencies to thwart terrorist activities is becoming a business necessity. Those that voluntarily join the government's efforts will continue to prosper. Those that don't will end up with costly delays and disruptions in their business activities.

3. *Make the most of new security measures.* By employing better practices with regard to security, your company will likely benefit from increased efficiencies

and lowered costs. Better inventory management, increased accountability, documentation accuracy, and tightening controls can all result in benefits to bolster your company's bottom line.

4. *Secure your data.* Take affirmative steps to manage data vulnerabilities by investing in comprehensive security solutions, restricting sensitive data, initiating vigilant employee screenings, and creating information management plans. The privacy and protection of customers' data is paramount in the cyber theft struggle and has become a competitive differential.

5. *Keep your personnel secure.* Initiate a crisis management plan to ensure the safety of your employees when overseas. Consider investing in K&R insurance and hiring security protection for employees and executives traveling in danger zones. Consult with the Overseas Security Advisory Council for information pertaining to government travel advisories and suggested security measures. When it comes to ensuring the safety and survival of your team, an ounce of prevention is worth a pound of cure.

EXPECT THE UNEXPECTED

No matter how sound your strategic plan and how prepared you are to move forward with your international business endeavors, there will come a time when circumstances beyond your control thwart even the best laid plans. Whether the issue is a natural disaster that disrupts distribution channels, an outbreak of influenza that can shut down commerce, worker strikes that close down ports, currency crises that turn a region's economy on its head, or a surprise coup d'etat in the country where you just opened a new factory, the longer you are involved in international business the more likely it is that some issue will arise that was unanticipated and unplanned. The smart global entrepreneur always expects the unexpected and has a flexible enough infrastructure to change course when circumstances dictate.

CRISIS IN PARADISE

Mention the Fiji Islands and the image of a South Pacific tropical paradise with pristine beaches, glorious waterfalls, nd dense rain forests probably comes to mind. While an accurate description of the 300-island archipelago, Fiji has historically also supported a bustling garment manufacturing sector. In fact, by the end of the past century, the garment industry employed more than a quarter of the country's workforce and operated more than 100 factories that exported clothing to Australia, the United States, Europe, and New Zealand. By 2001, apparel represented over 25 percent of Fiji's total exports and had overtaken sugar as its biggest export sector. Hopes were high that by 2005 exports of textile, clothing, and footwear products would hit the landmark figure of FJ$1 billion (nearly US$600 million) and support as many as 30,000 jobs.[1] During the 1990s, several of our firm's clients, looking for an efficient and cost-effective alternative to apparel production in high-quota cost markets such as China, set up factories in Fiji. The future looked bright for the industry.

Then, in May 2000, Fijian nationalists who opposed the ruling People's Coalition, a multiracial group dominated by the predominantly Indo-Fijian Labor Party, stormed parliament and held the prime minister, parliamentarians, and their staffs hostage for 56 days. Fighting erupted in the streets and the country was thrown into chaos. Backed by the military, the Fijian president denounced the coup and declared a state of emergency, imposing martial law. The uprising wreaked havoc on the country's infrastructure. There were power shortages, incidents of looting, and problems safely transporting employees to work. Many of the formerly profitable apparel factories were forced to close their doors as a result of the coup.

Fiji's history, like that of many of the developing countries where corporations source their production, is scattered with similar uprisings. In fact, there was another such incident in Fiji in December 2006 as this book was going to press. But of course the timing of these events is wholly unpredictable, and in 2000 none of the manufacturers operating factories in Fiji foresaw the political turmoil. Fortunately, our clients were able to quickly relocate production to plants in other parts of Asia and still meet customer demands. Those who did not maintain production centers in other locations were less successful.

PREPARING FOR THE WORST

Even though security to thwart acts of terrorism is at the forefront of every global trader's mind, there are a multitude of other disasters that can bring international business to its knees. A good rule of thumb for global traders is to plan for the worst—always. If it is unexpected, it will happen.

No matter how carefully you map out a sound business strategy, research your options, dot your i's and cross your t's, if you engage long enough in the international arena, eventually an unforeseen disaster of mammoth proportions—be it a political coup; labor unrest; the collapse of a country's currency; a natural disaster such as a hurricane, earthquake, or tsunami; or a worldwide pandemic—will frustrate your intentions.

On the heels of security measures, disaster preparedness has become an integral part of international business. While no plan can contemplate every contingency that can occur during a political uprising or natural disaster, global traders are well advised to plan for the worst. Recent events such as the West Coast port shutdown, the Mexican currency crisis, and Hurricane Katrina can provide valuable lessons in how to deal with catastrophe. In addition, the threat of a worldwide bird flu pandemic has international business interests scrambling to put sound disaster preparation plans in place. A review of each of these events highlights the consequences of the unexpected.

West Coast Port Lockout

The 29 ports spanning the U.S. Pacific coastline from San Diego to Seattle shut down for 10 days in the fall of 2002. The lockout by marine facility operators left importers, exporters, and shippers scrambling to execute contingency plans amid predictions that the closure would cost the U.S. economy as much as $1 billion a day.

With annual wages ranging from $80,000 to nearly $160,000,[2] longshoremen working at the ports along the United States' West Coast were enjoying good incomes and benefits in 2002. But that was no guarantee against labor unrest. Ports around the world were in the throes of modernizing their operations with advanced technologies like computers and scanners to track the movement of shipping containers, and West Coast terminal operators and shipping lines were feeling the need to follow suit in order to stay competitive. The International Longshore and Warehouse Union (ILWU) representing dockworkers did not dispute the need for modernization to boost productivity, but it insisted that the resulting jobs be given to union workers, a position that put it at odds with the dockside employers that made up the Pacific Maritime Association (PMA).[3]

The brewing threat of a labor dispute and the resulting blow it would inflict on the U.S. economy was readily apparent to the Bush administration. When new contract negotiations between the ILWU and the PMA began in mid-May 2002, the White House convened a working group to monitor the talks, and a Labor Department official stayed on top of the issue with regular phone calls to the involved parties throughout the summer. Homeland Security Director Tom Ridge warned ILWU president James Spinosa that the administration would intervene aggressively to stop a strike and cited several options: invoking the 1947 Taft-Hartley Act to force union employees back to work, using military troops to work the docks, enacting legislation to severely restrict dockworkers' ability to strike, or forcing the union to negotiate separate agreements at each port rather than a single contract covering the entire West Coast.[4] All of the options had one main goal: to keep cargo moving.

The close federal scrutiny was not surprising given that West Coast ports accounted for approximately 7 percent of U.S. gross domestic product at the time. According to government figures, these ports handled $300 billion in goods annually and supported 1.4 million jobs.[5]

Throughout the summer of 2002, the ILWU began to hold demonstrations against some of the stevedoring companies. Employers, in turn, were making accusations of work slowdowns by the union members and threatened a lockout. Shippers began to seriously consider alternative ports as a strike seemed imminent. Anticipating that the ports would close, on June 14 a senior executive representing a major carrier issued a statement offering to send shipments to East Coast ports, a costly proposition especially for shipments originating in Asia. Rerouting container vessels through the Panama or Suez canal posed problems of limited space, longer voyages, and higher costs, and the official noted that East Coast dockworkers could well refuse to unload diverted cargo in solidarity with their West Coast brethren. Plans were made to reroute some shipments to Vancouver, British Columbia, but there were concerns that Canadian longshoremen might boycott the vessels as well.[6]

The contract between the ILWU and the PMA expired July 1, 2002, but the union agreed to keep working while negotiations on a new contract continued. With virtually no progress by summer's end, the PMA ordered a lockout of all West Coast ports September 27.[7]

The lockout quickly resulted in a backup of cargo across the Pacific. It was the height of the peak season for imports from Asia, with $1 billion to $2 billion worth of cargo leaving Asian ports each day to fill retailers' holiday orders. With no dockworkers to unload the vessels, many were forced to anchor offshore, stranding tens of thousands of containers of consumer goods and industrial inputs. The situation was watched closely by manufacturers in Asia, who rely on shipments to the U.S. West Coast for about 5 percent of the continent's annual gross domestic product.[8]

As the lockout reached its fourth day, importers kicked into high gear their efforts to avoid the West Coast. Chiquita made plans to divert 180,000 boxes of bananas from Guatemala that had languished off the coast of Long Beach for three days to the Mexican port of Ensenada, where they would be loaded on trucks to ship across the U.S. border.[9] Airfreighting became an expensive option that some businesses had no choice but to take. Delaying shipments of perishable products and just-in-time parts would have cost even more in lost sales, stagnant production, and factory shutdowns. The impact of the lockout was felt up and down the supply chain. If the situation wasn't resolved quickly, fears were that a crisis would occur in Asian currencies and U.S. financial markets.

As the port shutdown entered its second week, pressure for federal intervention mounted. A group of 70 organizations representing farmers and agricultural businesses sent a letter to President Bush in early October asking him to reopen the ports. Four Republican lawmakers from Nebraska—Sen. Chuck Hagel and Reps. Doug Bereuter, Tom Osborne, and Terry Lee—also appealed to the president, saying, "If allowed to continue, this labor dispute will have a devastating ripple effect on all sectors tied to America's farm economy. Meat packers may soon be forced to drastically reduce the amount of livestock and poultry they process. Rail shipments of wheat and other grains to the Northwest have already been halted due to the lockout."[10]

In the end, the ports were closed down for 10 days. President Bush invoked the Taft-Hartley Act to end the lockout,[11] marking the first time that law had been used since President Jimmy Carter used it to break a coal miners' strike in 1978.[12]

Even after the longshoremen were back on the docks, the ripple effect of the work stoppage lingered for at least six weeks as retailers and manufacturers scrambled to free the backlog of cargo. With about 200 ships waiting to unload at the 29 ports that had been closed, companies were forced to wade through thousands of containers to decide which items to prioritize, then had to find trains and trucks to rush the merchandise to retail stores and manufacturing plants.

The Mexican Peso Takes a Dive

U.S. and European automakers were chomping at the bit to get a piece of the Mexican market following the implementation of the North American Free Trade Agreement (NAFTA) in 1994. General Motors, Ford, and Chrysler had shipped 60,000 vehicles to Mexico, up from fewer than 10,000 in 1993. The Big Three were gleefully anticipating an even bigger surge in Mexican sales for 1995. The future looked bright not only for these companies, but for Japanese and European auto companies who were likewise poised to penetrate the emerging Mexican market.

Then, a series of events in 1994—including political assassinations, an insurgent uprising, and a historically high economic deficit—culminated in newly elected President Ernesto Zedillo's decision to devalue the peso by 15 percent, resulting in catastrophe for the Mexican economy. Following the devaluation in December 1994, many foreign investors began pulling out of Mexico. By March 1995, the peso had collapsed to about seven pesos per dollar, a 51 percent drop.[13] With the country's gross domestic product decreasing by 6.2 percent in 1995, the resulting economic consequences were severe.[14] Experts predicted that the subsequent recession would result in 40 to 50 percent inflation, a significant decline in wages, widespread unemployment, and soaring interest rates.[15]

Mexico's economic situation in 1995 left the world's automakers scrambling to respond to plummeting new vehicle sales. With a population fast losing buying power and car loan interest rates skyrocketing to more than 40 percent, new car sales plunged 70 percent from a year earlier.[16]

Responding to the crisis, Chrysler announced plans to export nearly all of its 120,000 Mexican automobile inventory originally destined for the Mexican market. The Dodge Stratus, which Chrysler had produced specifically for the Mexican market, was reengineered for the American market, a tricky, time-consuming, and costly endeavor.

Nissan also suffered. In the first quarter of 1995, industry analysts estimated losses to the company as a result of the peso devaluation to be $300 million.[17]

Volkswagen, also hard hit by the crash, saw Mexican sales plummet by 85 percent. However, the German automaker was uniquely positioned to limit its losses. In January 1995, it halted production in Mexico for one week.[18] Then it shifted to the U.S. market thousands of Jetta sedans and Golf compact cars it had intended to sell in Mexico. This was relatively easy for the company to do since it already wholly served the U.S. market for those cars from its Mexican factories.[19]

As trade within Mexico came to a virtual standstill, the devalued peso proved to be a boon to the Mexican export market, especially as the United States began phasing in the duty reductions mandated by NAFTA in January 1994. After the peso's devaluation, exports in 1995 jumped up 31 percent in value, and more than 61 percent of the increased exports were destined for the United States.[20]

U.S. agriculture took a hard hit from this turn of events. U.S. exports of fresh fruits and vegetables to Mexico fell sharply in 1995, and the economic recession in Mexico contributed to a large increase in U.S. imports from Mexico in 1995 and 1996. U.S. tomato farmers were hardest hit by this import surge. By the end of January 1995, just over a month after the peso devaluation, Mexico had increased its share of the U.S. tomato market to 64.2 percent, compared to 42.9 percent a year earlier. During one week in February 1995, Mexican producers shipped 81.5 percent more tomatoes than the same period in 1994, compared with a 52.4 percent drop during the same period for Florida tomato shipments.[21]

The automakers were affected by an unanticipated turn of economic events in a market that they had counted on for business success. Was it reasonable to assume the promise of NAFTA would prove a boon to their business? Of course. Nevertheless, unforeseen political events affecting Mexico's developing economy resulted in severe disruption to the automakers' business plans. Even Volkswagen's tactical innovation in realigning its products for another market must have been a costly endeavor.

The Florida tomato growers found themselves in an untenable situation following the Mexican economy debacle. NAFTA proved clearly not to be a friend to this industry, which lost significant market share as a result of this turn of events. Even industries supposedly not intimately involved in a country's economic woes can be affected, evidencing that globalization truly is far-reaching, and every business must keep apprised of events happening around the world even if the effects may not be readily apparent.

Acts of God—Hurricane Katrina

We have become keenly aware how quickly natural disasters can ravage the global landscape. In the past decade, we've watched earthquakes, hurricanes, fires, floods, and tsunamis destroy societal, structural, and economic infrastructures within the space of a few hours.

On August 29, 2005, Hurricane Katrina made landfall on the northern Gulf Coast of the United States as a Category 4 hurricane. What would go into the history books as one of the worst natural disasters in U.S. history had a catastrophic effect on the cities of Mobile, Alabama; Gulfport and Biloxi, Mississippi; and New Orleans, Louisiana. The strong storm surge caused a breach of the levees separating Lake Pontchartrain from New Orleans, resulting in the flooding of nearly 80 percent of the city. The $75 billion in damage made Katrina the costliest hurricane in U.S. history, while the 1,836 storm-related fatalities made it the deadliest U.S. hurricane since 1928.[22] Federal relief efforts were estimated to reach upward of $200 billion.[23]

Katrina also exacted a heavy toll on large parts of the nation's distribution systems. More than 6,000 oceangoing ships carry millions of tons of agricultural products, commodities, and other goods every year to and from New Orleans and the other Louisiana ports that were shut down for days or weeks after the storm.[24] In 2004, these ports handled 61.5 percent of the soybeans, 63.9 percent of the corn, 44.3 percent of the rice, and 22.2 percent of the wheat exported from the United States.[25] The Midwest farmers that grow these crops rely heavily on the Mississippi barge system to transport them to ports in the New Orleans area for export, but in the aftermath of the hurricane the river was shut down, stranding hundreds of barges. There were few feasible alternatives to the slow but cheap barges: rerouting shipments to other ports would have required thousands of rail cars or tractor-trailers, which not only are more costly but also were in short supply due to the peak holiday shipping season.[26]

The nation's rail lines were also dealt a blow because New Orleans acts as a major rail center linking carriers of freight between the East and West Coasts. Trucking companies were unable to bring goods into or out of the city due to the widespread destruction of highways and bridges.[27]

Imports were affected as well, although to a lesser extent. New Orleans and its surrounding ports are some of the few in the entire United States that have the specialized equipment needed to transfer bulk goods and commodities from barges to the ships that carry them to overseas markets.[28] But other Gulf Coast ports are equipped to handle the oil, gas, steel, and containers of consumer and industrial products that make up the majority of imports through the lower Mississippi region, which they did while the relatively minor damage to terminal facilities there was repaired and ship channels were redredged.[29] Not all importers were as fortunate, however, particularly those dealing with perishable food products. At the port of Gulfport, Mississippi, for example, the refrigerated warehouses that handle imports of fruits and vegetables from Latin America were completely destroyed, forcing importers to reroute shipments to other ports with limited facilities to handle them.[30]

Pandemics and the Global Climate

Like natural disasters, pandemics too can change the world as we know it within days. Influenza pandemics are particularly virulent—and rapid. The "Spanish flu" of 1918 killed an estimated 50 to 100 million people around the world, including 675,000 in the United States in a six-month span.[31]

In 2003, the threat of the spread of severe acute respiratory syndrome (SARS) sent a shockwave around the globe. This deadly virus spread to more than two dozen countries in Asia, North America, South America, and Europe within a matter of months. While less than 800 deaths were reported before the World Health Organization determined in July 2003 that the outbreak had ended,[32] the effect on global trade and travel was immense just the same. Toronto, a metropolis of over five million, had a relatively mild outbreak that resulted in the deaths of a few dozen people, but even so the city became a virtual ghost town.[33]

A client of ours was in Hong Kong during the SARS outbreak there and was one of the few guests of the Regent Hotel. He told me that he had never felt so pampered and catered to, which is saying a lot given that the Asian standards for hospitality are very high. With few other guests to attend to, he truly felt like he was being treated like a king. The normally hustling and bustling streets of Hong Kong seemed deserted. One of the most vibrant business capitals of the world seemed to have emptied. Business meetings that had been scheduled were cancelled. Businesspersons from Europe, America, and other parts of Asia postponed or cancelled trips as they decided not to risk exposure to the virus. The consequent delays in placing orders and finalizing deals caused factory disruptions that translated into lost sales.

With today's world population hovering around 6.5 billion people, even a mild global pandemic could result in dire consequences. And we're not just talking lives. An influenza pandemic could have broad global economic, social, and security consequences. Mass transportation, the service industry, travel and tourism sectors, and health and security systems could be seriously disrupted in the wake of a pandemic. The World Bank reports that a pandemic's economic consequences could cost the global community an estimated $800 billion a year.[34] U.S. economic output could decline by over 4 percent.[35]

Avian influenza virus or bird flu has become the world's major flu pandemic threat in recent years. Although the virus is chiefly found in birds, infections can occur in humans.[36] Experts predict that the spread of this particular virus could trigger a reaction that would cripple entire economies and "change the world overnight."[37]

Think about it: Our global community consists of a tightly knit network of 70,000 transnational corporations and about 700,000 affiliates and subsidiaries—all of which rely on crossborder trade and travel.[38] But trade and travel will come to an abrupt halt in an attempt to stop the virus from entering new borders. As states and countries attempt to curtail the spread of the disease, transportation systems will be curtailed—severely affecting the distribution of medical supplies, food, and other necessary products and services.[39] Global growth is likely to slow precipitously, causing a worldwide recession. Prices for real estate and commodities would decline significantly and stock markets could crash.[40] World production would reach a virtual standstill.

Despite all of these warnings, a 2006 survey by an American pharmaceutical company found that 75 percent of American businesses do not have a contingency plan to counter the potential effects of an avian flu outbreak.[41] Those who are studying the situation believe that a contingency plan is essential to the survival of any business.

PLANNING FOR DISASTER

Can those engaged in transnational businesses ensure that they will never experience fallout from manmade or natural disasters? Of course not. There will always be circumstances and contingencies that are beyond your control. But smart global traders must add disaster preparedness, along with a sound security plan, into their business mix. By expecting the unexpected, global business can incorporate the basic principles of preparedness to minimize the impact of an unexpected disruption in the flow of trade.

There are numerous proprietary software programs, consultancy groups, and government guides that outline specific advice for disaster planning. Many, however, are not geared toward operations that cross continents. In many instances, the global trade professional must take these basic rules for emergency management one step further. The complexity of moving parts and personnel across borders during a crisis can be immense. If your primary supplier is an ocean away and you rely on its inputs or production will come to a standstill, you need to develop alternatives that will keep your business up and running. In the event of a port shutdown, alternative-shipping plans must be made. If your offshore operations are forced to close down, do you have other facilities that would be able to pick up the slack?

The details of your particular disaster preparations depend on your products, the countries in which you do business, and your internal and available external resources. The following list, however, provides some guidance for all global traders in formulating a disaster plan:

◆ Tailor your plan to focus on the vulnerabilities associated with your company's types of operations and physical locations. Coordinate with each country's and community's government agencies and organizations. Review and update the plan as often as needed to reflect changes in company policies, procedures, or operations; relevant laws and regulations; and economic and political events.

◆ Establish a concrete emergency response chain of command with clearly identified responsibilities.

Make sure each individual has the resources, equipment, and training necessary to carry out assigned tasks.

◆ Ensure that critical operations can be restored as soon as possible. Back up essential files, records, and other information, whether on paper or stored electronically, and store them in a safe manner, such as at an off-site location. Designate an alternate work location or provide for flexible work arrangements, such as telecommuting or different shift times. Provide for continuity of management. Establish backups for electronic services such as websites, payroll, customer relations, technical support, and so on.

◆ Disseminate your emergency response plan to all employees and conduct training and drills as appropriate.

◆ Ensure the safety and provide for the needs of your employees and their families.

◆ Encourage employees to be prepared at home. Make arrangements for salary continuation. Consider offering counseling, day care, and other services.

◆ Ensure that your contracts with vendors, service providers, financial institutions, and others include provisions allowing for flexibility in case of unforeseen developments, particularly if you are procuring goods or services from a country or region prone to natural disasters or political or economic instability.

◆ Line up alternative sources of supply in advance. Be able to shift production to other facilities, either within or outside your existing supply chain.

◆ Be prepared to reroute your shipments. Know in advance what other ports are able to handle your demands, both in the United States and abroad, and become familiar with any location-specific requirements. Investigate options for using different modes—air, rail, truck, or sea.

♦ Anticipate the need to store inventory for an extended period of time. Border closures, transportation delays or stoppages, and reductions in sales and revenue may require you to obtain warehouse or other storage space at various points along your supply chain.

♦ Understand how disasters or incidents and responses to them may affect demand for your goods or services. Know which alternate markets are attractive and be ready to adjust production, transportation, contracts, and so on accordingly.

♦ Evaluate your product lines or service offerings for vulnerability to measures likely to be imposed in response to an incident (e.g., increased cargo inspections, travel restrictions, prohibitions or limitations on certain imports or exports).

♦ Become an active and compliant member of applicable national cargo security programs. These programs give you greater visibility into your supply chain so you can head off potential problems quickly. Participants may also be given first priority when cargo transportation resumes following a disaster or incident.

♦ Establish cooperative working relationships with local and, as appropriate, national governments through compliance with applicable laws, community involvement, and so on. Consider the types of governments present in the countries in which you operate and their likely responses to disasters or incidents.

♦ Keep detailed records of actions taken that are allowed during an emergency or its aftermath but may otherwise be prohibited to forestall potential litigation or administrative proceedings.

♦ Set aside adequate reserves to cover increased expenses to cover employee needs, higher sourcing or transportation costs, storage/warehouse fees, and other expenses. Regularly review and update insurance coverage to reflect threats, vulnerabilities, corporate changes, and other factors.

Tenets of Global Trade

1. *The unexpected will happen.* The longer you are involved in international transactions, the greater the likelihood that a natural or manmade disaster will disrupt your operations. Be flexible enough to change course when the need arises.

2. *Do your research now.* There is a vast amount of helpful information available to assist you with disaster preparedness and contingency plans. Look to the expert consultants, consider existing software solutions, and consult government guides. Get the information you need now, before you really need it.

3. *Address your particular circumstances.* Tailor your plan to focus on the vulnerabilities of your company's operations and locations. Understand in-country resources—both government and private—and set up relationships now, before disaster strikes. Line up alternative supply resources, logistics plans, and manufacturing sites and, above all, ensure the safety of your employees and their families.

ALL GLOBAL BUSINESS IS PERSONAL

E-mail and teleconferences are poor substitutes for the real relationship building that can only come with face-to-face contact. In global business, that means travel, lots of it. The farther apart you are geographically and culturally from your offshore counterpart, the more important it is to meet face-to-face. Familiarity breeds good business relationships and fosters trust and mutual reliance that will spell success. When operating from your home base, be sure to make yourself available to your overseas associates at any time of the day or night. International business is not a 9-to-5 undertaking.

GLOBE-TROTTING AND RELATIONSHIP BUILDING

A few years ago, I found myself scheduled for a two-week trip that taxed even my high tolerance for frenetic business travel. But taking the time and trouble to show up for clients, business associates, and colleagues is critical to success in international business.

First, I flew from my home base of Miami to New York to meet with officials from the Israeli and Egyptian governments. The purpose of this meeting was to discuss the facilitation of a new trade program that had been created under the auspices of the Israel-U.S. Free Trade Agreement. The Egyptian Qualifying Industrial Zone (QIZ) program encourages business cooperation between Israeli and Egyptian manufacturers. The idea is that areas are established within Egypt where Israeli-provided materials are made into finished products (e.g., apparel or electronics) in the Egyptian zones. These finished goods can then be imported into the United States free of duty. The program is designed to not only offer U.S. importers the opportunity to purchase goods at reduced cost, a savings that can then be passed on to the American consumer, but also to bolster the Egyptian economy and facilitate cooperation between Israel and Egypt, two countries whose relationship has historically been, to say the least, volatile.

Sandler, Travis & Rosenberg had played a significant role in helping the Egyptian Exporters Association convince the U.S. government to sign off on a meaningful program. This face-to-face meeting with Egyptian and Israeli officials was part of the process of ensuring that transitioning from authorization to implementation of this remarkable program would accomplish the goal of furthering Egyptian/Israeli cooperation. While in New York, I also made a presentation to major apparel executives who had expressed interest in the program. This was not only an opportunity to tout a program that my firm had been instrumental in implementing, but it was also an opportunity to make contact with existing clients and new prospects.

From New York, I flew to Memphis to discuss international market facilitation in Latin America, and then took off for Las Vegas to present the keynote address in front of 200 executives attending a global sourcing exposition. Then it was back to Washington, DC, for a meeting of the Department of Homeland Security's Advisory Committee on Commercial Operations of Customs and Border Protection and Related Activities to discuss new security measures designed to protect our country from terrorist threats. Senior officials from the Department of Homeland Security and U.S. Customs and Border Protection participated in the meeting, along with representatives from the private sector. Following this meeting, I hopped on a plane to Milan to meet representatives of the gold jewelry industry to offer advice on ways to help them increase their competitive edge through tariff reductions on U.S. imports of jewelry. I then headed to Cairo to meet with 250 Egyptian entrepreneurs and representatives of the Egyptian government for further talks about implementation of that country's QIZ program. Because the Egyptian QIZ program relies on the establishment of joint ventures between Israel and Egypt, while in Cairo I also took the time to meet with Israeli businessmen who were investing in Egyptian apparel manufacturing facilities before heading back to the States to attend the annual meeting of the American Apparel and Footwear Association. Next stop was Haiti to work with industry executives on maneuvering trade legislation. The two-week whirlwind trip wound down in Little Rock, Arkansas, where I worked with Wal-Mart's sourcing group to relay the latest updates on global trade developments impacting the sourcing of soft goods like shoes and sports apparel.

THE IMPORTANCE OF FACE TIME

In today's world of lightning speed telecommunications, taking airplane after airplane to traverse continents just to give a couple of seminars and speeches, attend a few meetings, and work on some client development might seem like a waste of time and money. Why go to the expense and trouble of traveling when my law firm has invested in a state-of-the-art telecommunications infrastructure that is designed to support and enhance our ability to conduct worldwide communications? Wouldn't phone calls, e-mail, and videoconferencing (we are even set up to do "webinars," seminars that can be conducted and attended from the comfort of your desktop) provide enough of an appearance of personalized interaction to accomplish the same purpose at a much lower cost? The answer is this: *Nothing* compares with the time-tested up-close-and-personal approach to relationship building. A firm and friendly handshake, a welcoming smile, and a few hours of good old-fashioned "face time" is worth a thousand e-mails and videoconferences. There is simply no substitute for the energy that emanates from two individuals standing face-to-face, sizing each other up, and, more important, forming a personal bond. This is particularly true when you are developing relationships in locales far from your home office. In fact, the farther apart you are culturally and geographically from your business counterpart, the more important it is to show up in person.

The CEOs and COOs I have worked with over the years don't travel just for the sake of traveling. Most of them have been everywhere and there is no glamour in coping with jet lag, unappealing airplane food, the inevitable delays, and the other not-so-pleasant aspects of international travel even if you are flying on your own corporate jet. They get on a plane because that is what it takes to seal the deal, promote their firm, or embrace new opportunities. They know that, contrary to the famous line from *The Godfather* where mafia kingpin Vito Corleone explains that "It isn't personal, it's just business," *all business really is personal*. And nowhere is this more true than when forging international business relationships, where you must interact with strategic partners, clients, customers, and even members of your own offshore team across geographic and cultural divides. In my experience, the most successful global business transactions are always based on well-developed personal relationships. The time and effort you put into bridging geographic and cultural gulfs through personal interaction will come back to you 10-fold in business success. This is true whether you are a multinational corporation opening up an office in a new overseas location, a mid-size consultancy pursuing your first transnational venture, a consumer products company exploring offshore outsourcing, or a small company or sole proprietorship seeking new opportunities abroad. When it comes to forming new business relationships overseas, size really doesn't matter. The same rules that work for the largest multinationals hold true for the smallest companies.

Trust and Mutual Reliance

Opportunities abound in international business. But you must be willing to go to the source when seeking them out. The type of teamwork that is needed to turn vision into reality is always forged through personal relationships that foster an environment of trust and mutual reliance.

Back in the early 1990s, Sara Lee Knit Products, one of the world's leading producers of intimate apparel with brands such as Hanes and Playtex, was interested in creating partnerships in Central America to enhance its competitive edge by sourcing products directly from the region. As discussed in Chapter 2, Sara Lee has always thought outside the border when it comes to creating new opportunities to reduce costs without compromising quality and high on the agenda was creating a fabric-making facility in Central America to further this purpose. Sara Lee was actively seeking a willing and able partner who shared the company's vision. The then-senior executive of Sara Lee was Jack Ward, who undertook the task of making this vision a reality. And key to his plan was finding a willing and able partner, a fellow stakeholder, to share the risks and rewards of the endeavor.

Jack headed to Honduras to meet with a gentleman named Juan Canahuati, a major apparel producer in that country. Juan had a similar strategic vision for his company. He wanted to move into a more vertically integrated operation and to do that he needed to build a textile mill that would produce fabric in Honduras.

These two apparel manufacturing powerhouses sat down together and in just a few hours were able to understand each other's vision. They formed a partnership based on that shared vision and, more important, on mutual reliance. Each would have to make a significant contribution to the project for it to work. By sharing the stakes, they knew they could trust one another to give the endeavor their best efforts. And they knew that with their best efforts, success would be assured.

This type of business synchronicity fueled by a meaningful partnership has at its core a mutual trust based on personal relationship. Both companies needed to come together with a combined vision, which could only be realized when two individuals in positions of authority committed themselves and their respective companies to the mission. The key to the inevitable success of the Honduran textile mill was the face-to-face interaction between the business leaders. When forming a significant alliance of any type, e-mails and telephone calls are not enough.

This story has a wonderful epilogue. Years later, Jack Ward left Sara Lee to run another large clothing company, Russell Athletic, one of the leading activewear companies in the world. The Juan Canahuati mill still produces fabric for other companies but has added a slew of additional customers to its roster, including, of course, Russell Athletic. The partnership the two men formed developed into a long-term friendship that enhanced their business relationship in ways they never anticipated when they first came together. Fifteen years after that mill was created, these two giants of the apparel industry are still business associates working together under an umbrella of mutual reliance. And they are still friends.

DO WHATEVER IT TAKES

Strong leadership on both sides of the ocean is needed for success. And this leadership must extend to your offshore counterpart so that all parties to a venture are working in cooperation toward a mutually beneficial goal. By keeping the lines of communication with your offshore counterpart open, you develop a mutual understanding of how the two of you will work together to resolve problems.

When someone at an executive level, a level of authority and leadership, takes the trouble to travel across an ocean for a meeting, it sends out two important signals. First, it lets the individuals in his or her own company know that this is a serious matter that deserves their support and attention. Second, it signals to the overseas contact that you are willing to do what it takes to make the business venture work.

Of course, like Rome, that Honduran textile mill wasn't built in a day. Obviously, it took more people than just Jack Ward and Juan Canahuati to turn discussions about establishing a mill in Honduras into the actual realization of that enterprise. A lot of elements and scores of people had to come together for the strategic vision of two leaders to be realized. And you can bet that there were plenty of hurdles to jump over along the way. What Juan and Jack established was mutual trust and an agreement about a common goal—CEO to CEO. They had formed a strategic partnership, a marriage of sorts. They were both firmly committed to seeing their vision reach fruition. It was then up to a whole slew of individuals down the corporate chain to do the nuts-and-bolts work to make the vision a reality. You can be assured that there were operational, bureaucratic, even communications problems along the way, problems that in another context could have delayed or even killed the deal. In the end, no matter how powerful a particular player in a company is, forming a successful business venture overseas always boils down to a dependence on individuals that could be halfway around the world. Unless there is a mechanism for resolving problems based on a basic understanding between the companies and their respective leaders, it is going to be very hard to resolve problems when the bureaucracy gets involved because the level of commitment down the chain of command might not be that high. Mid- and lower-level managers perceive the risk/reward differently than the leaders. It's easier for associates at the lower levels to say no to something, to develop an impasse, to adopt a "we're sticking to our bible and you're sticking to your bible" mentality. But because Juan and Jack had developed a relationship and an open line of communication, they had formed a safety valve where each had a high level of confidence that nobody from either side was going to stand in the way of success with this venture. They kept their eyes on the prize and were ready to sit down whenever it was necessary to iron out the difficulties.

KEEP THE HOME FIRES BURNING

Business challenges can present themselves at any time. And Murphy's Law suggests that as soon as the wheels on that flight to Hong Kong lift off the runway, some crisis or another will occur at the home office. It is crucial that you have a team of trusted partners, dependable lieutenants, and a dedicated staff that is capable of handling whatever issues might arise on the home front while you are away.

As any executive who travels internationally a good deal of the time will attest, the freedom to pursue business interests abroad without worrying about how the home office is faring in his or her absence is of paramount importance. One of the keys to succeeding as a global entrepreneur is to set up the infrastructure of the home office so that it runs smoothly during your extended absences. Regular check-in times with your headquarters is of course crucial, but it is even more important that you leave the day-to-day operations in the hands of a trusted partner or lieutenant who can keep the home fires burning while you are away. Micromanaging your business in between meetings, or as you race through airports or cope with spotty Internet access from Third World hotel rooms, is not an efficient management technique. You need to have your "A" players at the helm of the home office so you are free to focus on your overseas endeavors.

SHOWING THE FLAG

By the same token, if you have established branch offices overseas, it is important to staff them with your best and your brightest managers. Being an expatriate business executive is not easy, and this is especially true if your foreign office representative is placed in a location that is at best lacking the creature comforts of home and at worst potentially dangerous. Always be sensitive to the needs of your expat partners and develop resources and assistance to make transitions smooth, especially if your foreign office staff bring family members with them.

It's also important to visit your foreign offices regularly to show the flag and give them that feeling of connection to the main office. But most important, choose your most trusted colleagues to staff your overseas office. Issues and problems can be plentiful when operating an offshore enterprise, especially in the developing world. You need your best and your brightest—the people who are able to operate independently and make crucial decisions on the fly when necessary.

THE PERSONAL TOUCH

One of the main reasons to meet with clients, suppliers, and customers face-to-face is to let them get to know you as a person, rather than just a business representative. While forming a personal level of relationship in business is certainly helpful in any industry, it is critical if you are a service provider. Lawyers, accountants, marketing and public relations specialists, systems consultants, and other individuals in the business of selling their services are also in the business of selling themselves. The "product" in this context isn't a three-dimensional widget or a manufacturing process, but the individual. So it stands to reason that the more you can relate to your offshore counterpart on an individual level, the more you stand to gain from the relationship. And when that counterpart is a continent away, selling yourself means crossing both geographic and cultural barriers.

When the Egyptian exporters first approached Sandler, Travis & Rosenberg to talk about engaging our services in furtherance of the QIZ agenda, the head of the group insisted on meeting with the leaders of the firm before sealing the deal. Sandler, Travis & Rosenberg came to the table with an excellent reputation for achieving results in these types of engagements and the Egyptian Exporters Association as a whole was behind the decision to hire us. But Galal al Zorba, the head of the association and also the president of a successful Egyptian apparel company, Nile Clothing, wanted to see just who these advisors were who were about to be entrusted with this important mission. He wanted to see what we were really made of.

The QIZ had been authorized by the U.S. Congress back in 1996 but political issues outside the control of Israeli and Egyptian businessmen had delayed its implementation.

Moving ahead with the program had its political sensitivities and Galal needed to size us up personally to make sure that we were up to the task. He wanted to make sure that the firm's leaders were fully behind the project and that we understood how important success was to his country and to him personally. He was putting his own reputation on the line and he wanted to look us in the eye and see if we were the kind of people he could trust. As managing partner of the firm, I immediately got on a plane and met with Galal and his associates in Egypt.

People feel a need to size each other up in business. They need to know: Who am I dealing with? Is this person credible? Is this the type of person I want representing my interests? The best way for potential clients to size you up is to see you in action, to see you across the table in different contexts, perhaps giving a speech or providing information to a group of clients. They want to see you on their home turf. They want to test you to see if you're suited for the job. It is the difference between providing a snapshot of someone or watching his starring performance in an action-packed motion picture. Your resume, brochure, website, and even long-distance interactive communications such as e-mails don't tell the whole story of who you are. The personal meeting provides the missing pieces and lets you show your best qualities.

Clients and potential business partners want to see how you will react to other people not related to business. How do you treat the wait staff at a restaurant? Or the receptionist at the company? A few years back, I took a young associate to Asia to meet with an important prospective client. My associate had just joined the firm and this was his first trip overseas. The client invited us to a Chinese banquet at an upscale Hong Kong restaurant.

This young attorney was just a few years out of law school and had not been exposed to an authentic Asian dining experience before. When he was offered chopsticks at the restaurant, he had the self-confidence to admit he was a bit chagrined at the prospect of eating with the traditional utensils. He politely, and a little sheepishly, asked the waiter for a fork. Later that evening, the young lawyer apologized to me profusely believing that his lack of worldliness had been an embarrassment for the firm. I let him know that after the banquet our host had taken me aside to comment the young associate had done exactly the right thing in trying to be himself. Two days later, we successfully concluded our business in Hong Kong. Of course, this associate became an expert in chopsticks etiquette prior to any subsequent trips to Asia.

MAKE YOURSELF AVAILABLE 24/7

International business is not a 9-to-5 endeavor. Stay close to your offshore business associates and be willing to work out any issue, any problem, at any time. The willingness to forego a little sleep here and there will reap big gains in solidifying important overseas relationships.

Any time you are dealing with an individual or organization in a different country or a different time zone, you have to make it clear that you are reachable any time, any place. I subscribe to a mobile telephone service with international reach and give the number out to all my clients. My mobile phone number is even printed on my business cards. I carry a Blackberry and check my e-mail throughout the day. And my executive assistant knows how to find me no matter where I am in the world and has strict instructions to track me down whenever necessary.

Recently, I was enjoying a Sunday night dinner with two of my grown children. We all have busy lives and getting two of my four children together for a quiet family dinner took weeks to plan. As soon as our entrees came my cell phone rang. It was a call from Singapore. The gentleman who called me was the head of the Singapore Textile Apparel Fashion Association and someone with whom I had developed a friendship over the years. The association had retained Sandler, Travis & Rosenberg to help them get an amendment to the Singapore-U.S. Free Trade Agreement. He was calling because he wanted me to set up a panel of industry experts for a conference I was to speak at in Singapore. I had offered to speak at the conference for free and here he was calling me on a Sunday night to request that I do additional work for them at no charge. The contract with the association was already signed and sealed so taking his call during a Sunday night dinner and agreeing to the additional work wasn't going to reap any immediate benefits for me or the firm. But being the go-to guy on these types of things is important in establishing trust and reliability for clients who are so far away. Of course, I interrupted dinner to take the call and agreed to help out with the panel. That is how international business is done. You always take the call, even if it's a Sunday night and you are having dinner with your kids.

On occasion, the calls come in the middle of the night. I was awakened at 4 A.M. not too long ago by a call from Beijing. A client of ours had to resolve some issues regarding ongoing negotiations between the United States and China. Quantitative restrictions on imported textiles and apparel had just been lifted worldwide, but the United

States was posturing to reimpose some restrictions on certain items from China. My client's business would be greatly affected by the outcome of these government-to-government talks and he was about to walk into a 4 P.M. meeting that could impact those proceedings. He knew that 4 P.M. in China was 4 A.M. in Miami, but he picked up the phone anyway because he knew that I would answer and that I would understand that he urgently needed to get in touch with me.

My clients feel secure that if they need me for anything, I am available any time of the day or night. And while it has been my experience that overseas clients are very aware of the time differences and will make every effort to avoid middle-of-the-night (for me) calls, occasionally the phone does ring at three or four in the morning. But it has only happened when the matter was urgent. And I know that the clients have always appreciated the fact that I was there for them, even at the expense of a good night's sleep.

While being jolted out of bed to answer a middle-of-the-night call or having Sunday dinner interrupted is fairly rare, the phone often rings at 11 or 12 at night, typically during the morning hours of the Asian businessman's workday. These nighttime calls are to be expected. It's part of the cost of doing business around the world.

You might find yourself in the same position from time to time. Perhaps a new overseas supplier will need to contact you for crucial last minute instructions. Or a new customer might need to change the specifications for an order in process. Whatever the issue, whatever the reason for the call, try to be as available and responsive as possible. Never let time zones or distance interfere with getting the job done.

Tenets of Global Trade

1. *Go to the source.* Opportunities abound in international business, but you must be willing to go to the source when seeking them out. The best business is always forged by establishing personal relationships, which in turn foster an environment of trust and mutual reliance.

2. *Keep communications open.* Strong leadership on both sides of the ocean is needed for success. Keep the communication channels open with your offshore counterpart and develop an understanding at the outset as to how problems will be resolved. Be sure to communicate down the corporate chain that nothing but success is acceptable.

3. *Keep the home office operational.* Make sure that trusted partners or top lieutenants are left at the helm of the home office when you are away. Attempting to micromanage headquarters while trying to do deals a continent away will distract you from the task at hand. Find trustworthy people and then leave them to do their jobs.

4. *Fly the flag at your overseas locations.* Select your best and your brightest to staff your overseas operations and make regular visits to show the home office's support. Ensure that expatriate employees and their families are well taken care of and kept safe. Nobody can command a field office if they are worrying about the safety or comfort of their loved ones.

5. *Relate to offshore associates on a personal level.* People need to size each other up in business. Don't be afraid to let clients and customers get to know you as a person, rather than just a business associate.

6. *Be available to overseas clients and customers 24/7.* International business is not a 9-to-5 job. Be available to your offshore associates to handle any issue at any time.

TRANSPARENCY AND THE TENETS OF GLOBAL TRADE

In the preceding chapters, I've discussed a number of ways that your company can maximize its chances of succeeding in the global marketplace today and into the future. I termed these principles for success the *Tenets of Global Trade* because they apply to virtually every international enterprise. While the tenets can be seen as separate and distinct, there is one underlying element that serves to bind them into a cohesive protocol for international business. That element is *transparency*. The modern business environment demands that companies involved in international trade not only ensure that their own operations are able to withstand scrutiny by investors and regulators, but that they also push this culture of openness all the way back down their supply chains.

As a global trade entrepreneur, you have an obligation to become intimately familiar with all the players on your team, and it is equally important that they know you. When operating a business that crosses multiple borders, there will inevitably be miscommunications, mistakes, and misunderstandings. If you lose visibility into your global supply chain and fail to communicate effectively with strategic partners, consultants, customers, and clients, it will be next to impossible to promote commonality of purpose and to ensure that all the players are effectively working together. If you allow the various pieces of the global trade puzzle to spin out of your orbit, it can be extremely difficult to regain the level of alignment that is so important to the oversight of complex multicountry transactions. If you can't see a problem you can't fix it. And if your strategic partners can't reach out to you easily to stave off problems before they materialize, then you lose control of the process. Transparency is a two-way street. All parties to an international transaction must have access to important transactional information.

TRANSPARENCY: THE FUTURE IS NOW

As I thought about the Tenets of Global Trade and how to introduce the concept of transparency as a significant element that permeates each tenet, I was brought back to the fantastic success of Wing Tai and its dynamic management team led by the ever-innovative and forward-thinking Christopher Cheng.

In Chapter 1, I related the story of how my 1994 breakfast meeting with Cheng in Hong Kong started an incredible series of events that culminated in Cambodia's gaining the coveted U.S. most-favored-nation status and subsequently becoming an Asian apparel production powerhouse. I also pointed out how the textile quota agreement Cambodia entered into with the United States set off a series of chain reactions affecting international labor standards by setting the stage for a new paradigm for the inclusion of labor provisions in subsequent U.S. trade agreements. Through my firm's ongoing interactions with Wing Tai and the personal relationships I have developed with not only Cheng but a number of that company's executives, I have continued to bear witness to the company's contributions to the evolution of trade innovation. So it should come as no surprise that as I contemplated how best to relate where I see the future of trade progressing and sought to introduce the importance of transparency in all aspects of global trade that I would again look to Wing Tai to point me in the right direction.

In its development as an international apparel company with more than 20 manufacturing operations in many different countries and numerous customers in Europe and the United States, Wing Tai found itself in need of a state-of-the-art systems approach that would meet its changing needs as well as those of its customers and contractors. This need for a sophisticated system that tracks the production of merchandise from purchase order to manufacture to the retail sales rack had become of paramount importance in the international apparel business. Ever at the cutting edge of new developments, Wing Tai went in search of the perfect business solution.

The company's needs were well-defined. Customers were demanding more visibility throughout the production process. This was a reaction to both quality control and internal process requirements, and the need to improve efficiencies in inventory management and distribution. It was also because Wing Tai's customers were seeking an antidote to the increase in government requirements concerning security and trade program verification. Wing Tai was determined to give its customers exactly what they needed—detailed production records that trace the flow of product development from design to the fabric mill to the cutter to the maker to the finisher to the packer and through each subsequent transportation point until the garments reach the store shelves. Wing Tai's quest would not end until it had achieved a mechanism for complete transparency in the production process.

The president of Wing Tai Apparel, the innovative and creative Steven Walton, led his team on an exhaustive search for a tracking system that would allow this level of detail in production visibility. In the end, the results of the search for a third-party provider with a comprehensive solution were disappointing. While different providers offered discrete pieces to monitor production, none broke down the entire process in the way that Wing Tai's customers demanded: stitch by stitch, SKU by SKU. Walton and his associates rolled up their inventors' sleeves and set out to create a system the likes of which had never been contemplated before.

During the course of this search, Walton happened upon a company called Texwatch and its master of software solutions, Vincent Chan. Along with Ivy League credentials, Chan came from an apparel-producing family. He had the domain knowledge to understand the issues and the technical expertise to produce tangible results. Together, Chan and Walton approached Christopher Cheng. Their idea? They would build the mother of all apparel-processing transparency tracking solutions themselves.

MSC Limited was born, with Chan at the helm as CEO. Developed initially for Wing Tai's own internal use, MSC's products are now an integral part of the operating structures of some of the world's most recognized branded apparel companies. And the company constantly evolves its offerings to meet the needs of a changing trade community.

MSC's supply chain monitoring system is truly ahead of its time. Instead of approaching apparel manufacturing as a vertical endeavor with a supply chain that travels upstream, MSC saw that the industry has become increasingly horizontal. End products emanate from what MSC terms a "core enterprise," a manufacturer or trading company that has formed strategic alliances both upstream and downstream. The horizontal nature of modern-day manufacturing encompasses global suppliers, manufacturers, and distributors. Inside each of these enterprises, trade flows, products flow, information flows, and capital flows. MSC sees the new globalized trading landscape for what it is, a far-reaching and diverse environment in a world that, although flat, is still quite large and oftentimes incongruous.

MSC addresses these incongruities by offering transparency at all stages of the manufacturing process. Through the integration of new technologies such as Radio Frequency Identification (RFID), which allows for specific component tracking down to the level of individuals working the production line, up through the production process to the incorporation of systems solutions that provide a single information platform, MSC is able to create an end-to-end supply chain window.

The fact that an innovator like Wing Tai would spin off a company like MSC is ample proof that transparency and global trade are forever intertwined.

Transparency and Trade Agreements

The first Tenet of Global Trade we discussed was Take Advantage of Trade Agreements. No global entrepreneur should be without a thorough knowledge of the agreements and preferences that affect his or her product or market. But as is often the case, the devil is in the details, and nowhere is this more true than when putting processes in place to conform to the detailed requirements of trade program eligibility.

A U.S. importer desirous of importing electronics, apparel, or heavy machinery duty-free under NAFTA, for example, must be able to track the origin of each item on its bills of material to prove that any applicable requirements such as regional value content and place and manner of processing meet the agreement's detailed conditions. If a single manufacturer along the supply chain unilaterally changes operations without the stakeholder's prior consent or without a thorough knowledge of the potential repercussions to the free trade agreement (FTA) requirements, disaster can result.

Recently, a client contacted Sandler, Travis & Rosenberg because U.S. Customs had disallowed a claim under the Dominican Republic-Central America Free Trade Agreement (DR-CAFTA). One of this client's suppliers had found a deal on sewing thread that significantly lowered its costs. While purchasing less-expensive thread may have seemed like a good idea from a procurement standpoint, this decision ended up costing our client a lot of money. The cheaper thread was sourced from a disallowed country and use of the thread in the imported garments threw the entire shipment out of DR-CAFTA program eligibility. The goods were now dutiable and our client lost any hopes of realizing its sales margins. Incredible as it sounds, even seemingly insignificant factors like the origin of thread must be a factor in supply chain transparency.

Customs officials, tasked with protecting U.S. revenue, are more vigilant than ever in enforcing the provisions of programs that afford duty breaks. Keeping detailed records, filling out eligibility forms properly, and being prepared to back up any statements you make with evidence of the veracity of your claims is a prerequisite to enjoying the benefits of any trade program. Without absolute transparency, you subject your company to not only the loss of the duty benefits but also penalties and, in some instances, even criminal prosecution of company officials.

Transparency as a Tool to Protect Your Brand and Promote Ethical Practices

Adhering to the second and third Tenets of Global Trade—Protect Your Brand At All Costs and Maintain High Ethical Standards—also requires a high degree of transparency. Your intellectual property—your patents, copyrights, and trademarks—are some of your company's most valuable assets. Each time you license your intellectual property to a third party or engage a factory to produce goods carrying your logo, you are taking a risk that your mark will be misused or misappropriated. The only way to monitor this important asset is by establishing a system of transparency through contractual arrangements and regular monitoring. As I pointed out in Chapter 3, counterfeiting and pirating are rampant throughout the world. And while no self-monitoring system will guarantee total brand protection, it is almost assured that without making your best efforts in this regard, you will end up seeing poor-quality counterfeit goods bearing your intellectual property in the marketplace.

The other important manifestation of your brand, your company's overall reputation among the consumer public, can only be protected if you take care to keep ethics high on your corporate agenda by employing sound corporate governance protocols.

Companies can no longer look the other way when unscrupulous contractors operate in sweatshop conditions or wreak environmental havoc. Non-governmental organizations and private watchdog groups, government-sponsored organizations such as the United Nations' International Labor Organization, and hard-hitting investigative reporters stand ready to expose any acts of corporate malfeasance. Bribery, noncompliance with international trade rules and regulations, and engaging in other illegal or immoral behavior can affect your company's financial future and even impact the freedom of its principals. Transparency in operations is the only way to ensure that your company does not run afoul of its own ethical dictates. Written ethics policies, self-monitoring programs, and publication of your business partners and contractors are sound ways to infuse transparency into your operations in order to avoid both the act and the appearance of impropriety.

Transparency and Security

In Chapter 5, I introduced the fourth Tenet of Global Trade: Stay Secure in an Insecure World. Security, especially in a post 9/11 world, has become synonymous with transparency. Detailed information surrounding the origin of inbound cargo must be transmitted to the appropriate Customs officials in advance of arrival, a requirement that can only be met if transparency is present. Supply chain transparency has become mandatory for U.S. importers and is fast becoming a requirement for importing in ports throughout the world. Because the government cannot possibly inspect every cargo shipment that enters U.S. ports, the onus is now increasingly on global entrepreneurs to carefully monitor supply chain activities. To ensure that a container holding your goods is not hijacked by international terrorists and turned into a conveyance for weapons of mass destruction, you must be able to trace your goods as they progress in production from inception to delivery. Solutions to closely monitor all facets of the supply chain, such as that created by MSC and those offered through our firm (see the following discussion), are invaluable tools in your company's anti-terrorism arsenal.

Increasingly, governments are requiring importers to prove up front that they have sufficient internal controls and procedures to thwart any attempts to breach cargo security. Cooperation between government and private business is the key to keeping borders secure from terrorism and, increasingly, the private sector is under an ever-greater obligation to help in the international war against terrorism. Through programs like the Customs-Trade Partnership Against Terrorism (C-TPAT) and U.S. Customs' Importer Self Assessment (ISA) program, importers are expected to prove that their transactions have complete transparency by mapping out and self-monitoring every stage of production. And, as previously discussed, the ancillary benefits of incorporating strong internal controls and procedures throughout the supply chain include increased efficiencies, decreases in waste and redundancies, and the potential for cost savings as a result.

Transparency as Preparation for the Unexpected

As discussed in Chapter 6, all global traders should prepare for unanticipated contingencies. In other words, they should adhere to the next Tenet of Global Trade and Expect the Unexpected.

Transparency plays a role in readying your company to handle contingencies such as currency crises, political instability, labor unrest, and natural disasters. In this context, transparency becomes an internal issue. Each member of your team, up and down the chain of command, must understand the enterprise's drills when it comes to acting fast to thwart the effects of surprise problems and issues that affect the flow of business. By keeping your options open and your alternatives transparent, you are assured that every member of your team has his or her marching orders and can quickly react to whatever crisis presents itself.

Being a Transparent Global Entrepreneur

Transparency is even a necessary element of the final Tenet of Global Trade: All Global Business Is Personal. This tenet is predicated on my personal belief, based on my own experiences, that nothing replaces the intimacy of personal contact in business relations. In essence, you are making yourself transparent to your offshore strategic partners. By letting them know who you are, what you can do, and that you are available to them 24/7, you engender an atmosphere of trust and mutual reliance. And this can only be accomplished by breaking down cultural and geographic barriers and opening yourself up in a personal way. I am proud to say that many of my clients have over the years become good and trusted friends. And without this added element of transparency, I don't believe that these mutually beneficial business and personal relationships would continue to thrive.

PRACTICING WHAT WE PREACH

As I conclude this book, I think it is important to empha- size that I have applied many of the lessons I have reported on to my own global business. The Tenets of Global Trade and their relationship to the emergence of transparency as an essential element of global trade have provided the im- petus for the evolution of both my law firm, Sandler, Travis & Rosenberg, and its related consulting firm, Sandler & Travis Trade Advisory Services (STTAS).

Ten years or so ago, the United States embarked on a concerted push toward encouraging free and open trade. Reflecting this proliferation of new trade agreements and an overall increase in trade, STTAS developed a propri- etary software system called TradeVIA™ and created a managed services division that allows importers to address the need for transparency and compliance throughout the supply chain.

TradeVIA is a systems-based tool that protects the in- terests of international business by providing visibility, regulatory compliance, and security-related transparency to import and export transactions. The system allows importers to outsource critical import compliance and recordkeeping functions to increase efficiencies, lower costs, and maximize the duty-savings benefits of trade programs. Using TradeVIA, STTAS analysts can classify merchandise under the harmonized tariff sched- ule of any country, track certificates of origin and other

documentation needed to prove trade program or preference eligibility, and manage bills of material. To promote
compliance with security transparency requirements, the
system integrates advance manifest requirements, export
and import compliance, and inventory management, and
even tracks C-TPAT participation requirements. For the
companies using the system—ranging from the world's
largest automakers to branded apparel companies to electronics manufacturers—TradeVIA, in conjunction with
STTAS' managed service offerings, effectively manages
the daunting tasks of substantiating NAFTA and other
trade and preference program eligibility while promoting
compliance with government-mandated security measures. We preach to our clients that trade agreements
provide unmatched opportunities for global business success. Therefore, it seemed natural that we would create
this management and information tool, which provides
transparency and enhances compliance, to assist them.

Because security compliance is at the forefront of
every global trader's mind, STTAS has developed a program specifically designed to assist with C-TPAT compliance. The Global Security Verification Program (GSVP) is
an independent inspection and analysis tool developed in
response to demand from importers and suppliers seeking
a cost-effective solution to verify compliance with
C-TPAT security criteria. The GSVP accomplishes this
goal by providing onsite verifications of existing security
measures, an analysis of these security measures against
C-TPAT criteria, and a detailed report of actions necessary to improve security and maintain C-TPAT compliance. The GSVP tool is identical to the program used by
the U.S. government in assessing C-TPAT compliance and

provides a global third-party verification that focuses on pinpointing holes in transparency within the global supply chain. Again, this expansion of service offerings into the security arena reflects the growing importance and primacy of security for those who strive for success in the global marketplace.

We have stressed the importance of ethics in doing business globally and the need for transparency to enforce appropriate standards of conduct. Paralleling this development, we created a corporate social responsibility group within the law firm to assist companies in defining their principles and creating and implementing programs to ensure that they comply with both the law and their own internal standards. With a former deputy under secretary of labor at the helm of the firm's labor practice, Sandler, Travis & Rosenberg professionals provide an assessment of the labor laws and regulations in countries in which clients plan to do, or are already doing, business. Next, the firm assists clients to develop and implement codes of conduct and compliance programs tailored to specific needs. Should problems arise, Sandler, Travis & Rosenberg acts as an advocate in remedying deficiencies.

As the landscape of global trade evolves, STTAS and Sandler, Travis & Rosenberg are continually creating new service offerings in response to the needs of companies in complying with the many responsibilities set forth in this book. And as our clients expand their operations, we have heeded their calls to export our services to meet their evolving needs. We have opened a South American office in Sao Paulo and an Asian arm based in Beijing to better address the global reach of our multinational clients. We are working with the U.S. government in the development of its customs modernization protocols through STTAS' participation in the Automated Commercial Environment (ACE) development project. And we have developed a software tool known as eGrid to assist customs departments and other entities around the world responsible for international trade to better manage risks with respect to valuation fraud, money laundering, narcotics smuggling, weapons of mass destruction, and other health and safety threats.

As to the future of global trade, all indications point to an even greater increase in accessible markets and a concomitant need for sensible, cost-efficient solutions to facilitate the free flow of goods across borders. It is my belief that the Tenets of Global Trade set forth in this book are universal and timeless in application. They are valuable tools of the trade and, as my 30 years in the industry can attest, will stand the test of time.

NOTES

CHAPTER 2: TAKE ADVANTAGE OF TRADE AGREEMENTS: THINK OUTSIDE THE BORDER

1. Interactive Tariff and Trade Dataweb, U.S. International Trade Commission, http://dataweb.usitc.gov (accessed October 2006).
2. Office of the U.S. Trade Representative, 2006 *Comprehensive Report on U.S. Trade and Investment Policy Toward Sub-Saharan Africa and Implementation of the African Growth and Opportunity Act,* May 2006, http://www.ustr.gov/assets/Document_Library /Reports_Publications/2006/asset_upload_file236_9455.pdf.
3. Office of the U.S. Trade Representative, "Andean Trade Preference Act," http://www.ustr.gov/Trade_Development /Preference_Programs/ATPA/Section_Index.html.
4. Office of the U.S. Trade Representative, "Free Trade Agreements Are Working for America," CAFTA Policy Brief, May 26, 2005, http://www.ustr.gov/assets/Document_Library /Fact_Sheets/2005/asset_upload_file204_7872.pdf.
5. U.S. Department of Commerce, "U.S.-Israel Free Trade Agreement: Fact Sheet," http://www.export.gov/fta/Israel /fact_sheet.asp?dName=Israel.
6. House Committee on International Relations, "Economic Development and Integration as a Catalyst for Peace: A

'Marshall Plan' for the Middle East," 107th Cong., 2nd sess., July 24, 2002, p. 125, http://commdocs.house.gov /committees/intlrel/hfa80963.000/hfa80963_0.htm.

7. Associated Press, "Egyptian-Israeli Trade Soars 130 Percent," *Israel Insider,* December 18, 2005, http://web.israelinsider .com/Articles/Briefs/7285.htm.

8. "About QIZ," QIZ Egypt, http://www.qizegypt.gov.eg/www /english/about/about_qiz_overview.asp.

CHAPTER 3: PROTECT YOUR BRAND AT ALL COSTS

1. Teresa McUsic, "From Handbags to 'Anything Made by Man,'" *Star-Telegram,* October 6, 2006, http://www.dfw .com/mld/dfw/news/15694080.htm.

2. Office of the U.S. Trade Representative, 2006 *Special 301 Report,* p. 5, http://www.ustr.gov/assets/Document_Library /Reports_Publications/2006/2006_Special_301_Review /asset_upload_file473_9336.pdf.

3. International Anti-Counterfeiting Coalition, "The Negative Consequences of International Intellectual Property Theft: Economic Harm, Threats to the Public Health and Safety, and Links to Organized Crime and Terrorist Organizations," white paper, January 2005, p. 10, http://www .iacc.org/resources/IACC_WhitePaper.pdf.

4. Joe McDonald, "Arrests in Fake Baby Formula Case," Associated Press, May 10, 2004, http://www.cbsnews.com /stories/2004/05/10/health/main616432.shtml.

5. World Health Organization, "Counterfeit Medicines," fact sheet no. 275 (revised February 2006), http://www.who .int/mediacentre/factsheets/fs275/en.

6. Frederik Balfour, "Fakes!" *BusinessWeek,* February 7, 2005, http://www.businessweek.com/magazine/content/05_06 /b3919001_mz001.htm.

7. Stephen M. Pinkos, Deputy Under Secretary of Commerce for Intellectual Property, "Piracy of Intellectual

Property," Senate Judiciary Committee Subcommittee on Intellectual Property, 109th Cong., 1st sess., May 25, 2005, http://www.ogc.doc.gov/ogc/legreg/testimon/109f/Pinkos052505.htm.

8. See note 5.

9. Sandler, Travis & Rosenberg, PA, "U.S. Announces Major New Initiative to Combat Global Trade in Counterfeit Goods," WorldTrade\Interactive, October 6, 2004, http://www.strtrade.com/wti/wti.asp·ub=0&story=1817&date=&searches=1&yellow_1=strategy%20targeting.

10. Office of the U.S. Trade Representative, "USTR Schwab Announces New Office Focused on Intellectual Property," press release, June 23, 2006, http://www.ustr.gov/Document_Library/Press_Releases/2006/June/USTR_Schwab_Announces_New_Office_Focused_on_Intellectual_Property.html.

11. U.S. Customs and Border Protection, "FY 2005 Top IPR Commodities Seized," L.A. Strategic Trade Center, November 3, 2005, http://www.customs.gov/linkhandler/cgov/import/commercial_enforcement/ipr/seizure/fy05_midyear_stats.ctt/fy05_ipr_midyear.pdf; and CBP, "Yearly Comparisons: Seizure Statistics for Intellectual Property Rights," http://www.customs.gov/xp/cgov/import/commercial_enforcement/ipr/seizure/seizure_stats.xml.

12. Tommy Hilfiger Corporation, "Global Labor Standards," http://usa.tommy.com/opencms/opencms/ethics.

13. Fred Tasker, "Kathie Lee: Sweetheart or Swamp Witch?" Milwaukee Journal Sentinel, www.findarticles.com/p/articles/mi_qn4196/is_19970616/ai_n10335786.

14. Verena Dobnik, "Kathie Lee Clothes Again Linked to Sweatshop Labor," Milwaukee Journal Sentinel, December 6, 1997, http://www.findarticles.com/p/articles/mi_qn4196/is_19971206/ai_n10387544.

15. "Kathie Lee Gifford," text of National Museum of American History exhibit on sweatshops, http://americanhistory.si.edu/sweatshops/dialogue/5t8.htm.

16. Democracy Now! "Kathie Lee Gifford Accused of Running Sweatshops in El Salvador," September 27, 1999, http://www.democracynow.org/print.pl?sid=03/04/07/0410227.

17. Steve Boggan, "Nike Admits to Mistakes over Child Labor," *The Independent,* October 20, 2001, www.commondreams.org/headlines01/1020-01.htm.

18. John H. Cushman Jr., "Nike Pledges to End Child Labor and Apply U.S. Rules Abroad," *New York Times,* May 13, 1998, http://www.corpwatch.org/article.php?id=12965.

19. See note 18.

20. See note 18.

21. John Robbins, "Is There Slavery in Your Chocolate?" The Food Revolution: How Your Diet Can Help Save Your Life and the World, http://www.foodrevolution.org/slavery_chocolate.htm.

22. See note 21.

23. See note 21.

24. Senator Tom Harkin, "Joint Statement from U.S. Senator Tom Harkin, Representative Eliot Engel, and the Chocolate/Cocoa Industry on Efforts to Address the Worst Forms of Child Labor in Cocoa Growing Protocol Work Continues," press release, July 1, 2005, http://harkin.senate.gov/news.cfm?id=240245.

25. The Hershey Company, "About the Hershey Company: Responsible Cocoa Growing," http://www.thehershey company.com/about/cocoa.asp.

26. See note 25.

27. Kerry Howley, "Absolution in Your Cup," *Reason,* March 2006, http://www.reason.com/0603/fe.kh.absolution.shtml.

28. Fairtrade Labelling Organizations International, "Generic Standards for Producers," http://www.fairtrade.net/producer_standards.html.

29. TransFair USA, "Starbucks Coffee Company Brings Fair Trade Certified Coffee to Retail Stores Through TransFair USA Alliance," press release, September 25, 2000, http://www.transfairusa.org/content/about/pr_000925.php.

30. Starbucks, "Corporate Social Responsibility Fiscal 2005 Annual Report," p. 4, http://www.starbucks.com/aboutus /FY05_CSR_Total.pdf

31. Amnesty International, *Clouds of Injustice: Bhopal Disaster 20 Years On* (London: Amnesty International Publications, 2004), http://web.amnesty.org/library/pdf/ASA200152004ENGLISH /$File/ASA2001504.pdf.

32. Union Carbide Corporation, "The Incident, Response, and Settlement," http://www.bhopal.com/irs.htm.

33. Union Carbide Corporation, "Statement of Union Carbide Corporation Regarding the Bhopal Tragedy," http:// www.bhopal.com/ucs.htm.

34. Environment News Service, "India Asks U.S. to Extradite Former Union Carbide Chairman," OneWorld.net, July 9, 2003, http://www.commondreams.org/headlines03/0709-09 .htm.

35. Responsible Care, "Who We Are," http://www .responsiblecare.org.

36. American Chemistry Council, "Tracking Performance, Sharing Results," http://www.chemicalguide.com.

37. William J. Clinton, "Remarks by the President to the Luncheon in Honor of the Ministers Attending the Meetings of the World Trade Organization," Seattle, Washington, December 1, 1999, http://usmission.ch/press1999/122clin .html.

38. Gary G. Yerkey, "Jordan Cracks Down on Firms Exploiting Foreign Workers in Violation of Trade Pact," *International Trade Daily*, Bureau of National Affairs Inc., July 7, 2006.

CHAPTER 4: MAINTAIN HIGH ETHICAL STANDARDS

1. Federal Bureau of Investigation, "News Release Summary" March 1, 2005, http://sandiego.fbi.gov/dojpressrel /pressrel05/titancorporation.htm.

2. U.S. Securities and Exchange Commission, "SEC Sues the Titan Corporation for Payments to Election Campaign of Benin President," press release 2005-23, March 1, 2005, http://www.sec.gov/news/press/2005-23.htm.

3. *Securities and Exchange Commission v. The Titan Corporation*, complaint, Civ. Action No. 05-0411 (R), United States District Court for the District of Columbia, March 1, 2005, p. 9, http://www.sec.gov/litigation/complaints/comp19107 .pdf.

4. See note 3, p. 13.

5. See note 2.

6. See note 1.

7. Thomas Donaldson, "Values in Tension: Ethics Away from Home," *Harvard Business Review*, September/October 1996, http://www2.gol.com/users/coynerhm/values_in_tension.htm.

8. Frank Vogl, "Curbing Corruption: Making Progress with the Bribe-Givers," *Economic Perspectives*, USIA Electronic Journal, vol. 3, no. 5, November 1998, http://usinfo.state .gov/journals/ites/1198/ijee/vogl.htm.

9. Alliance Bernstein Global Investment Research, "Evaluating the Impact of Corporate Governance Standards in the Emerging Markets," p. 4.

10. Carol Mates, "Recent Developments at IFC," remarks delivered at seminar on monetary and financial law, International Monetary Fund, Washington, DC, May 8, 2002; and IFC, "Corporate Governance and Capital Markets," http://www .ifc.org/ifcext/economics.nsf/Content/CG-Corporate _Governance_Department.

11. U.S. Securities and Exchange Commission, "Douglas Murphy and David Kay Receive Prison Sentences for Violating Foreign Corrupt Practices Act," litigation release no. 19293, July 6, 2005, http://www.sec.gov/litigation/litreleases /lr19293.htm.

12. U.S. Securities and Exchange Commission, "Douglas Murphy and David Kay Found Guilty of Violating Foreign

Corrupt Practices Act in Criminal Action Brought by Department of Justice," litigation release no. 18925, October 7, 2004, http://www.sec.gov/litigation/litreleases/lr18925 .htm.

13. See note 11.

14. Hannah Clark, "More Fraud Abroad," Forbes.com, April 4, 2006, http://www.forbes.com/2006/04/04/fraud -abroad -bribery-cx_hc_0405fraud_print.html.

15. International Chamber of Commerce, "Business Toughens Anti-Bribery Rules," press release, October 6, 2005, http:// www.iccwbo.org/policy/anticorruption/iccehch/index.html.

16. International Chamber of Commerce, "Combating Extortion and Bribery: ICC Rules of Conduct and Recommendations," 2005 ed., http://www.iccwbo.org/uploadedFiles /ICC/policy/anticorruption/Statements/ICC_Rules_of _Conduct_and_Recommendations%20_2005%20Revision .pdf.

17. Transparency International, "Business Principles for Countering Bribery," http://www.transparency.org/global_priorities /private_sector/business_principles.

18. United Nations Global Compact: "Transparency and Anti-Corruption," http://www.unglobalcompact.org/AboutTheGC /TheTenPrinciples/anti-corruption.html; "What Is the Global Compact?" http://www.unglobalcompact.org/AboutTheGC /index.html; and "Business against Corruption: A Framework for Action," 2005, http://www.unglobalcompact.org/docs /issues_doc/7.7/BACtextcoversmallFINAL.pdf.

19. Organization for Economic Cooperation and Development: "Promoting Corporate Responsibility: The OECD Guidelines for Multinational Enterprises," *International Investment Perspectives*, chapter 7, 2004, http://www.oecd.org/dataoecd /54/16/34896738.pdf; and *The OECD Declaration and Decisions on International Investment and Multinational Enterprises: Basic Texts*, Directorate for Financial, Fiscal and Enterprise Affairs, Committee on International Investment and Multinational

Enterprises, DAFFE/IME(2000)20, November 9, 2000, http://www.olis.oecd.org/olis/2000doc.nsf/4f7adc214b91a685 c12569fa005d0ee7/c125692700623b74c1256991003b517 /$FILE/00085743.pdf.

20. OECD: *Convention on Combating Bribery of Foreign Public Officials in International Business Transactions,* http://www.oecd.org /document/21/0,2340,en_2649_37447_2017813_1_1_1 _37447,00.html#text; and "Fighting Bribery in International Business Deals," policy brief, November 2003, http://www .oecd.org/dataoecd/2/58/20610942.pdf.

21. OECD, *Convention on Combating Bribery of Foreign Public Officials in International Business Transactions,* http://www.oecd.org /document/21/0,2340,en_2649_37447_2017813_1_1_1_ 37447,00 .html#text.

22. United Nations Office on Drugs and Crime, "United Nations Convention against Corruption," http://www.unodc .org/unodc/en/crime_convention_corruption.html.

23. U.S. Customs and Border Protection, "What Every Member of the Trade Community Should Know About: Recordkeeping," January 2005, http://www.cbp.gov /linkhandler/cgov/toolbox/legal/informed_compliance_pubs /icp027.ctt/icp027.pdf.

24. U.S. Department of Justice, "Caviar Company and President Convicted in Smuggling Conspiracy," press release, January 31, 2002, http://www.usdoj.gov/opa/pr/2002 /January/02_enrd_052.htm.

25. Bureau of Industry and Security, "Major Cases List," October 2006, http://207.96.48.13/ComplianceAndEnforcement /Majorcaselist.pdf.

26. Bureau of Industry and Security, "Don't Let This Happen to You: Actual Investigations of Export Control and Antiboycott Violations," May 2006, http://207.96.48.13 /ComplianceAndEnforcement/Dont_Let_This_Happen_To _You_2006.pdf.

27. See note 26.

28. See note 26.

29. Office of the U.S. Attorney, District of Minnesota, "Valtex International Corporation and Owner Plead Guilty to Felonies for Attempted Export to People's Republic of China," press release, February 2, 2005, http://www.bis.doc.gov/news/2005/ValtexAug_03_05 .htm.

30. Sandler, Travis & Rosenberg, PA, "Criminal Sentence Imposed on Exporter for Double Invoicing Scheme," client advisory, January 15, 2002, http://www.strtrade.com/default .asp?link=advisory.asp&id=31.

31. Sandler, Travis & Rosenberg, PA, "Exporters under Heightened Scrutiny for Valuation Discrepancies," *World-Trade\Interactive*, vol. 13, no. 182, September 12, 2006, http://www.strtrade.com/wti/wti.asp·ub=0&story=25524 &date=&searches=1&yellow_1=Brazil.

32. Crowell & Moring LLP, "Customs Tightening NAFTA Recordkeeping Requirements," *International Trade Bulletin*, June 12, 2006, http://www.crowell.com/ClientAlert/International/Crowell_ITB_All_6-12-06.html; and Susan Kohn Ross, "Customs Update: Record What?" *Journal of Commerce*, May 4, 2006, www.joc.com.

33. Levi Strauss & Co., "Levi Strauss & Co. Global Sourcing and Operating Guidelines," http://www.levistrauss.com /Downloads/GSOG.pdf.

34. See note 8.

35. Motorola Corporation, "Ethics & Code of Business Conduct," http://www.motorola.com/content.jsp?globalObjectId =75-107.

36. "Ethics Officers: A Growing Breed?" *Ethical Corporation*, February 7, 2005; and Ethics & Compliance Officer Association, "About the ECOA," http://www.theecoa.org /AboutECOA.asp.

CHAPTER 5: STAY SECURE IN AN INSECURE WORLD

1. Meredith Cohn, "Global Trade Group to Adopt Rules for Protecting Cargo," *Baltimore Sun*, June 23, 2005, http://www .baltimoresun.com/business/bal-bz.port23jun23,0,2454743 .story?coll=bal-business-indepth.

2. Angela Greiling Kane, "Cargo Theft Is Counted; and Provision in Patriot Act Establishes Cargo Crime Category, Boosts Punishments for Theft Convictions," *Traffic World*, March 20, 2006, http://www .cargosecurity.com/ncsc /ncsc_dotnet/articals/Cargo_Theft%20is%20Counted% 20032006%20Traffic%20World.pdf.

3. John Albrecht, "Security Strategies for Cargo Companies," http://www.securitymanagement.com/library/000505.html.

4. 19 USC §1584.

5. U.S. Customs and Border Protection, "Carrier Initiative Program (CIP)," http://www.cbp.gov/xp/cgov/border_ security/international_activities/partnerships/cip.xml.

6. U.S. Customs and Border Protection, "Business Anti-Smuggling Coalition (BASC)," http://www.cbp.gov/xp /cgov/border_security/international_activities/partnerships /basc.xml.

7. U.S. Customs and Border Protection, "Americas Counter Smuggling Initiative (ACSI)," http://www.cbp.gov/xp/cgov /border_security/international_activities/partnerships/acsi .xml.

8. Barchi Peleg-Gillai, Gauri Bhat, and Lesley Sept, *Innovators in Supply Chain Security: Better Security Drives Business Value*, The Manufacturing Innovation Series (Washington, DC: The Manufacturing Institute, July 2006), http://www-1.ibm.com /businesscenter/cpe/download28/60833/InnovatorsSupply Chain.pdf.

9. Peter Branton, "On the Defensive," ITP Technology, September 3, 2006, http://www.itp.net/features/details.php ?id=5017&category.

10. Associated Press, "Ameriprise Notifies Clients of Data Theft," USAToday.com, January 26, 2006, http://www.usatoday.com/money/perfi/general/2006-01-26-ameriprise-ap_x.htm.

11. Carrie Kirby and Jenny Strasburg, "40 Million Cards Hit by Data Theft," *San Francisco Chronicle*, June 18, 2005, http://www.sfgate.com/cgi-bin/article.cgi?file=/c/a/2005/06/18/CREDIT.TMP.

12. Greg Sandoval, "Veterans' Data Swiped in Theft," CNET News.com, May 22, 2006, http://news.com.com/Veterans+data+swiped+in+theft/2100-1029_3-6075212.html.

13. "AT&T Computer Systems Hacked," *Red Herring*, August 30, 2006, http://www.redherring.com/Article.aspx?a=18264&hed=AT%26T+Computer+Systems+Hacked&sector=Industries&subsector=Computing.

14. Robert Lemos, "Bank of America Loses a Million Customer Records," CNET News.com, February 25, 2005, http://news.com.com/Bank+of+America+loses+a+million+customer+records/2100-1029_3-5590989.html.

15. Vontu Inc., "Ponemon Institute Releases National Survey on Confidential Data at Risk," news release, August 15, 2006, http://www.vontu.com/news/release_detail.asp?id=532#Top.

16. Liz Pulliam Weston, "Your Financial Secrets are Headed Overseas," MSN Money, http://moneycentral.msn.com/content/Banking/FinancialPrivacy/P90682.asp.

17. IPLocks Inc., "Don't Be Blindsided from the Inside Out with Data Security Risks," http://www.technology-reports.com/report.asp?id=533.

18. Gregg Keizer, "Consumers Flog Firms that Lose Data," *TechWeb Technology News*, November 14, 2005, http://www.techweb.com/wire/173602532.

19. Ben Charny, "AOL Technology Chief Departs Over Data Gaffe," MarketWatch, August 22, 2006, http://www

.marketwatch.com/news/story/story.aspx?guid=%7BCA86
9F99-E81D-4EBF-ADC8-F9CBC67B2700%7D.

20. Kirk Semple, "The Kidnapping Economy in Colombia,"
New York Times Magazine, June 3, 2001, http://www
.criminology.fsu.edu/transcrime/articles/The%20Kidnapping
%20Economy%20in%20Colombia.htm.

21. Reuters, "Oil Workers May Leave Niger Delta," Aljazeera
.net, August 23, 2006, http://english .aljazeera.net/NR
/exeres/98137CE1-12FB-4E4B-B7D9-8CE95DF19E72.htm.

22. "A King's Ransom," *Economist*, August 24, 2006, http://
www.economist.com/finance/displaystory.cfm?story_id
=7843592.

23. See note 22.

24. Assurex Global, "Kidnappings for Ransom on the Rise,"
press release, June 1, 2001, http://www .assurex.com/main
.asp?show=news&go=press&id=24&type=archived.

25. See note 24.

26. Carol Patton, "Dangers Lurking: With Kidnappings on the
Rise, Companies Need to Become More Aggressive Securing the Safety of Employees Who Travel or Work Overseas," *Risk & Insurance*, October 1, 2004, http://findarticles
.com/p/articles/mi_m0BJK/is_12_15/ai_n6239818/pg_1.

27. See note 26.

28. Konrad Yakabuski, "Danger Pays," *Globe and Mail*, August 24, 2006, http://www.theglobeandmail.com/servlet
/story/RTGAM.20060824.rmgarda0824/BNStory
/specialROBmagazine/home.

29. Overseas Security Advisory Council, "About OSAC," http://
www.osac.gov/About/index.cfm.

CHAPTER 6: EXPECT THE UNEXPECTED

1. Donovan Storey, "The Fiji Garment Industry," Oxfam, http://
www.oxfam.org.nz/resources/Oxfam%20Fiji%20Garment
%20Study.pdf.

2. Nancy Cleeland, "White House Signals Move to Forestall West Coast Port Strike," *Los Angeles Times*, August 5, 2002, http://www.labournet.net/docks2/0208/bushilwu1.htm.

3. David Bacon, "West Coast Docks Fall Silent as Workers Are Locked Out," October 2, 2002, http://dbacon.igc.org/Unions/21Lockout.htm.

4. See note 3.

5. Nancy Cleeland, "White House Signals Move to Forestall West Coast Port Strike," *Los Angeles Times*, August 5, 2002, http://www.labournet.net/docks2/0208/bushilwu1.htm.

6. Gary Osterbach, "Industry Update 2: ILWU," *Danzas AEI Resource Newsletter*, no. 351, June 14, 2002, http://www.dgf.dhl.com/frameset.cgi?winLocation=http://www.dgf.dhl.com/worldwide/northamerica/resource/351.html.

7. See note 3.

8. Ilya Garger, "On the Waterfront," *Time* (Asia ed.), October 21, 2002, http://www.time.com/time/asia/magazine/article/0,13673,501021021-364420,00.html.

9. *Marketplace*, October 2, 2002, American Public Media, http://marketplace.publicradio.org/shows/2002/10/02_mpp.html.

10. Forrest Laws, "Port Strike Damage Spreading East," *Western Farm Press*, October 4, 2002, http://westernfarmpress.com/news/farming_port_strike_damage/index.html.

11. See note 8.

12. See note 5.

13. U.S. Department of Agriculture, Economic Research Service, *International Agriculture and Trade Situation and Outlook*, June 12, 1995, http://usda.mannlib.cornell.edu/reports/erssor/international/wrs-bb/1995/wrs95-2f.asc.

14. "Emerging-Market Indicators: Mexico," *The Economist*, February 19, 1998, http://www.economist.com/displaystory.cfm?story_id=604785.

15. See note 13.

16. Julia Preston, "Mexican Peso Fall Leads to Auto-Sales Standstill," *New York Times*, August 10, 1995, http://www .eco.utexas.edu/~archive/chiapas95/1995.08/msg00058 .html.

17. See note 16.

18. MexiNews, "VW Impresses Analysts," Global News Mexico, University of California San Diego, January 12, 1995, http://ssdc.ucsd.edu/news/mexico/h95/mexico.19950112 .html.

19. See note 16.

20. Library of Congress, Federal Research Division, "A Country Study: Mexico," call number F1208.M5828 1997, http:// lcweb2.loc.gov/frd/cs/mxtoc.html#mx0080; and U.S. Census Bureau, "Trade in Goods (Imports, Exports and Trade Balance) with Mexico," http://www.census.gov/foreign-trade /balance/c2010.html#1995.

21. "Kantor to Help Growers Review Import Surge Petition on Tomatoes," *Inside U.S. Trade*, March 10, 1995, www .insidetrade.com.

22. Jerry D. Jarrell, Max Mayfield, Edward N. Rappaport, and Christopher W. Landsea, "The Deadliest, Costliest, and Most Intense United States Hurricanes from 1900 to 2000," National Oceanic and Atmospheric Association, NOAA Technical Memorandum NWS TPC-1, updated October 2001, http://www.aoml.noaa.gov/hrd/Landsea /deadly/index.html.

23. Kevin Kennedy, "What the Weather Can Teach Us about the Unfair Trade Remedy Laws: The Lessons of Hurricanes Katrina, Rita, and Wilma," Occasional Papers in International Trade Law and Policy, no. 1, Institute for Trade in the Americas, Michigan State University College of Law, http://72.14.209.104/search?q=cache:IEcVD4ayir4J :www.law.msu.edu/ita/ITPSNo.1.pdf+kevin+kennedy +unfair+trade&hl=en&gl=us&ct=clnk&cd=1.

24. Janet Adamy, Paul Glader, and Daniel Machalaba, "Katrina Takes Her Toll on the Grain Traders," *Wall Street Journal*,

September 1, 2005, http://www.organicconsumers.org/Politics/krebs090705.cfm.

25. U.S. Bureau of the Census, Foreign Trade Division "Top 25 U.S. Exports and Imports by 6-Digit HS through the District of New Orleans, Based on 2004 Values," http://www.census.gov/foreign-trade/statistics/country/sreport/neworleans.txt.

26. See note 24.

27. Alexei Barrionuevo and Claudia H. Deutsch, "A Distribution System Brought to Its Knees," *New York Times*, September 1, 2005, http://www.nytimes.com/2005/09/01/business/01cargo.html?ex=1283227200&en=ae2a0308b49fba43&ei=5088&partner =rssnyt&emc=rss.

28. John Fritelli, "Hurricane Katrina: Shipping Disruptions," Congressional Research Service, September 13, 2005, http://digital.library.unt.edu/govdocs/crs//data/2005/upl-meta-crs-7619/RS22257_2005Sep13.pdf?PHPSESSID=adb7142bdaf303f18f8e0efe5f9bc7da#search=%22Katrina%20shipping%22.

29. See note 28.

30. See note 28.

31. U.S. Centers for Disease Control and Prevention, "Pandemics and Pandemic Threats Since 1900," http://www.pandemicflu.gov/general/historicaloverview.html.

32. U.S. Centers for Disease Control and Prevention, "Frequently Asked Questions about SARS," May 3, 2005, http://www.cdc.gov/ncidod/sars/faq.htm.

33. David Crosson, "Toronto Physicians Reveal Fears While Coping with SARS Outbreak," Health Behavior News Service, September 1, 2005, http://www.hbns.org/news/SARS09-01-05.cfm.

34. World Bank, "Avian Flu: Economic Losses Could Top US$800 Billion," press release, November 8, 2005, http://web.worldbank.org/WBSITE/EXTERNAL/NEWS/0,,contentMDK:20715408~pagePK:34370~piPK:34424~theSitePK:4607,00.html.

35. U.S. Congressional Budget Office, "A Potential Influenza Pandemic: Possible Macroeconomic Effects and Policy Issues," December 8, 2005 (revised July 27, 2006), p. 12, http://www.cbo.gov/ftpdocs/69xx/doc6946/12-08-BirdFlu .pdf.

36. U.S. Centers for Disease Control and Prevention, "Avian Influenza (Bird Flu)," http://www.cdc.gov/flu/avian.

37. Michael T. Osterholm, "Avian Flu: Addressing the Global Threat," testimony before the House Committee on International Relations, December 7, 2005, http://www .internationalrelations.house.gov/archives/109/ost120705 .pdf.

38. Gary Lamphier, "Bird-Flu Fears Bring up Debate over Global Risks," *Edmonton Journal*, June 1, 2006, http://www .canada.com/edmontonjournal/news/business/story.html? id=3d2cd16d-0066-4143-8ffe-d711bfc1e67b&k=21228.

39. See note 37.

40. See note 38.

41. "Pandemic Flu Preparedness Going Slowly in the U.S.," September 27, 2006, http://www.continuitycentral.com /news02807.htm.

INDEX